miracles

miracles
A JEWISH PERSPECTIVE

RONALD H. ISAACS

JASON ARONSON INC.
Northvale, New Jersey
Jerusalem

"Elijah the Builder," "Elijah and the Three Wishes," and "Miracles all Around" from *Jewish Stories: One Generation Tells Another*, by Peninnah Schram, Copyright © 1996 Peninnah Schram. Used with permission of the publisher.

"Opening Your Eyes" from *The Book of Miracles: A Young Person's Guide to Jewish Spirituality*, by Lawrence Kushner, Copyright © 1987 UAHC Press. Used with permission of the publisher.

This book was set in 12 pt. Goudy Old Style by Alabama Book Composition of Deatsville, Alabama and printed and bound by Book-mart Press of North Bergen, New Jersey.

Library of Congress Cataloging-in-Publication Data

Isaacs, Ronald H.
    Miracles : a Jewish perspective / by Ronald H. Isaacs.
        p.   cm.
    Includes bibliographical references and index.
    ISBN 0-7657-9950-2 (alk. paper)
    1. Miracles—Biblical teaching.   2. Bible.   O.T.—History of
Biblical events.   3. Miracles in rabbinical literature.   4. Legends,
Jewish.   I. Title.
BS1199.M5I83   1997
296.3'116—dc21   97-9519
                                                                  r97

Manufactured in the United States of America. Jason Aronson Inc. offers books and cassettes. For information and catalog write to Jason Aronson Inc., 230 Livingston Street, Northvale, New Jersey 07647.

Contents

Acknowledgments

Much of this book was written while working at Camp
Ramah in the Poconos, a beautiful place in the hilly forested
Pocono mountains, which in the last few years has become my
summer home. The beauty of this camp and its people have
always helped to inspire my writing. I am also forever indebted
to my professor Abraham Joshua Heschel, of blessed memory,
for reminding me to always lift up my eyes and truly "see" the
power, grandeur, and mystery of the amazing things in our
world. He has taught me never to take things in life for
granted.

Introduction

Have you ever witnessed or taken part in what you considered to be a miracle? Many people have. Whether they are psychic phenomena or encounters with spiritual healings, miracles can profoundly affect the way we view ourselves and our world.

Throughout Jewish history, there have been extraordinary events that have had a significant and lasting affect on the Jewish people. The parting of the Red Sea, the heavenly manna that descended in the desert, the cloud of glory, and Bilaam's talking donkey—just to name a few—certainly have become memorable biblical stories, which have greatly impacted upon the community of Israel and humankind in general. The Talmud, too, is replete with stories and legends of a wondrous nature. In medieval Jewish philosophy, the subject of miracles was one of the most important.

It is part of the richness of Jewish tradition that any one of these spectacular and remarkable experiences can mean different things to different people. Over the centuries, rabbinic thinkers and commentators have discussed these and other events in an attempt to define the exact nature of the miracle and how a Jew is to properly understand it. Their writings and comments provide the reader with an incredible array of thought-provoking material that can assist us in formulating our own opinions related to the subject.

This volume is intended to introduce readers to the variety of Jewish views relating to miracles. Material is drawn from several sources, including the Bible, Talmud, midrash, and Zohar.

I hope this volume will help you discover your own unique answers to life's eternal mysteries and to learn new ways to encounter and react to the sacred and wondrous occurrences in daily life.

Ronald H. Isaacs

What is a Miracle?

Extraordinary phenomena, distinguished from normal and usual events, are frequently referred to as miracles. In the ancient world, the miraculous was quite a popular thought-pattern, according to which God intervened in the ordinary course of events to express His will and purpose.

There is no biblical Hebrew word for "miracle." The closest related words are *wonder* (*mofet*) or *sign* (*ot*). Our ancestors regarded the miracles of the Bible as literally true and authentic. They did not differentiate between the natural and the supernatural, since it was the one omnipotent God that caused all to be and set the course of nature according to His will. Thus the dividing of the Red Sea and the manna from heaven were accepted as standard historical events, with the Bible itself making no reference to the miraculous nature of these happenings. In God's world there is nothing that is impossible.

Today, there are people who look upon miracles as inspiring allegory parables and metaphors, rather than actual historical events. Others have devoted extensive time in trying to find

1

natural explanations for the miracles of the Bible. Scientists studying the ten plagues during the Israelite slavery in Egypt have suggested that low tides and sudden winds may have resulted in the appearance of the Sea of Reeds splitting, while the darkness in Egypt was the result of some type of eclipse.

Of course, there are those more traditionalist thinkers who regard the rationalist's attempt to explain the biblical miracles in naturalistic terms as blasphemy. They contend that miracles are the work of an all-knowing omnipotent God. Humans, with their limited power of reason, can never fully comprehend the nature of a miracle. One must, they say, continue to have faith in God's ability to create a miracle when a particular occasion necessitates.

HIDDEN AND REVEALING MIRACLES

Judaism differentiates between the so-called hidden miracle and the revealing miracle. In rabbinic thinking, a hidden miracle is an occurrence that is so mundane that its wondrous nature is overlooked. Hidden miracles are taken for granted as normal events and not as supernatural ones.

Events that cannot be explained and that seem to defy the normal scheme of things have never been the major preoccupation of Jewish thinkers. Judaism and its thinkers have been much more interested in the "miracles" that are evident each day: the air we breathe, the fact that the sun rises and sets each day, the beauty of nature's creations (flowers, plants, streams, rivers, and lakes). Life itself is considered a hidden miracle, so often taken for granted until illness strikes.

In Jewish liturgical thought, God is viewed as constantly renewing the miracle of creation every day. In the daily prayer the Amidah (traditionally recited three times each day), we implore God to keep us mindful of the hidden miracle: "We give thanks and praise You morning, noon, and night for Your miracles which are with us everyday and for Your wondrous kindnesses."

The other type of miracle is the revealing miracle, a powerful, extraordinary sudden event that contradicts the normal scheme of nature. This is the kind of miracle in which it is believed that God supernaturally intervenes to change the normal course of events. Although Judaism does say that God is certainly capable of performing this kind of miracle, it discourages a person's desire for God to interrupt His own laws of nature. Instead, rabbinic thinkers have encouraged people to be cognizant each day of the countless miracles that are always with us and offer words of praise to God for His never failing power.

MIRACLES IN CHRISTIANITY

In contradistinction to Judaism's somewhat reserved attitude toward miracles and the rejection of them as affirmations of religious truths, miracles play a very important role in Christianity. The Gospels are a long record of miracles performed by Jesus. They range from demonstrating Jesus' control over nature such as the time he attended a wedding feast and changed the water into wine (John 2:1–11) to his control over the power of death as shown when he raised his friend Lazarus from the grave (John 11:17–44).

While Judaism refuses to acknowledge miracles as proof of divine authorization, the Gospels adduce the miraculous acts of Jesus as proof. Each miracle performed by Jesus was designed to reveal that Jesus held the power of God to perform such works, illustrating not only Divine authorization but his divinity itself. Even more significant, whereas Judaism has no dogmas involving the belief in miraculous terrestrial events, Christianity is predicated on numerous doctrines of this kind, including the incarnation of Jesus and the Virgin birth.

As a result of this emphasis on the supernatural, Christianity, especially in its Catholic form, has become, in a sense, enslaved to miracle stories. Catholicism chooses its saints on the strength of the miracles they perform.

As a result of the large part that miracles played in the early history of Christianity, Christian worship revolves around the mysteries of the sacraments, numbering seven in Catholicism and two in the Protestant confessions. Baptism and the Lord's Supper, the two sacraments recognized in all Christian denominations, are thoroughly imbued with miracle elements. Baptism is believed to clean the newborn from original sin. The Lord's Supper, the partaking of the Eucharist and the sacramental wine, are regarded as the establishment of a direct physical bonding between the believers and Jesus, of whose body and blood they symbolically partake by eating the Eucharist and drinking the wine of communion.

Judaism, on the other hand, has no sacraments. Jewish ritual knows of no prayer or sacrament through which salvation can be achieved through some miraculous means.

The following is a summary of the major miracles of Jesus and the references in the New Testament where they are found:

1. Changing water into wine (John 2:7–8)
2. Healing the nobleman's son (John 4:50)
3. Healing the Capernaum demoniac (Mark 1:25; Luke 4:35)
4. Healing Peter's mother-in-law (Matthew 8:15; Mark 1:31; Luke 4:39)
5. Catching many fish (Luke 5:5–6)

6. Healing a leper (Matthew 8:3; Mark 1:41)
7. Healing a paralytic (Matthew 9:2; Mark 2:5; Luke 5:20)
8. Healing a man with a withered hand (Matthew 12:13; Mark 3:5; Luke 6:10)
9. Healing a centurion's servant (Matthew 8:13; Luke 7:10)
10. Raising a widow's son (Luke 7:14)
11. Calming the stormy sea (Matthew 8:26; Mark 4:40; Luke 8:24)
12. Healing a woman with internal bleeding (Matthew 9:22; Mark 5:29; Luke 8:44)
13. Raising Jairus's daughter (Matthew 8:25; Mark 5:41; Luke 8:54)
14. Healing two blind men (Matthew 9:29)
15. Healing a dumb demoniac (Matthew 9:33)
16. Healing an invalid (John 5:8)
17. Walking on water (Matthew 14:25; Mark 6:48; John 6:19)
18. Feeding the five thousand (Matthew 14:19; Mark 6:41; Luke 9:16; John 6:11)
19. Healing a demoniac girl (Matthew 15:28; Mark 7:29)
20. Healing a deaf person with a speech impediment (Mark 7:34–35)
21. Feeding the four thousand (Matthew 15:36; Mark 8:6)
22. Healing a blind person at Bethsaida (Mark 8:25)
23. Healing a person born blind (John 9:7)
24. Healing a demoniac boy (Matthew 17:18; Mark 9:25; Luke 9:42)
25. Catching a fish with a coin in its mouth (Matthew 17:27)
26. Healing a blind and dumb demoniac (Matthew 12:22; Luke 11:14)

27. Healing a woman with an 18-year infirmity (Luke 13:10–17)
28. Healing a person with dropsy (Luke 14:4)
29. Healing ten lepers (Luke 17:11–19)
30. Raising Lazarus (John 11:43–44)
31. Healing a blind man of Jericho (Luke 18:42)
32. Healing blind Bartimaeus (Mark 10:26)
33. Withering the unfruitful fig tree (Matthew 21:19; Mark 11:14)
34. Restoring a severed ear (Matthew 26:51; Mark 14:47; Luke 22:50–51; John 18:10)
35. Catching a great number of fish after the resurrection (John 21:6)
36. The star in the sky that guided the wise men (Matthew 2:1–10)
37. Allowing Elisabeth to bear a son (Luke 1:6–13, 57)
38. The transfiguration of Jesus (Matthew 17:1–13; Mark 9:1–13; Luke 9:28–36; II Peter 1:16–18)
39. The resurrection (Matthew 28; Mark 16; Luke 24; John 20)
40. The ascension (Luke 24:50–52; Acts 1:4–11)
41. Blinding Saul (Acts 9:8)
42. Freeing Paul and Silas from prison (Acts 16:19–40)
43. The Calvary miracles:
    a. Darkness (Matthew 27:45)
    b. Earthquake (Matthew 27:51)
    c. Rent veil in the Temple (Matthew 27:51)
44. Rolling away the stone at Jesus' resurrection (Matthew 28:2)
45. Opening prison doors for disciples (Acts 5:19–23)
46. Freeing Peter from prison (Acts 12:1–17)

MIRACLES IN THE BIBLE

Remember the wonders He performed, His miracles. . . .
(Psalm 105:5)

The Bible is the oldest and most widely read book in our civilization. It has been in continuous circulation for almost two thousand years and has been the source of religious ideals and values for countless people. Ever since Sinai, perhaps the most wondrous event in all recorded biblical history, the moral imperatives of the Bible have provided a great spiritual heritage for all humankind. Today there are some people who look upon the Bible as a giant prayer book containing a long record of divine manipulations of Israel's early history. Others, with a more analytical bent, read the Bible as the world's most famous history book, whose accuracy continues to be demonstrated by archaeological findings and the corroborative evidence furnished by the histories of other Middle Eastern civilizations. Like the ancient histories of other nations, the Bible is interwoven with legends and reports of miraculous events. But what is a miracle to one observer or reader is a fortunate coincidence to another.

There is no biblical Hebrew word for miracle. The Bible uses words such as *peleh* or *mofet* which is often translated as a "wonder" or "marvel." In the Bible, almost every occurrence which contrasts with the routine happenings of life is counted as a miracle or wonder. God says in Exodus 3:20: "So I will stretch out My hand and smite Egypt with the various wonders which I will work upon them. After that, he shall let you go." Four chapters into the Book of Exodus (Exodus 7:3), God says to Moses: "I will harden Pharaoh's heart that I may multiply My signs and wonders in the land of Egypt." In Exodus 34:10, God provides one reason for His decision to work wonders with the enslaved Israelites in Egypt: "Before all your people I will work such wonders as have not been rendered on all the earth or in any nation. And all the people who are with you shall see how awesome are God's deeds which I will perform for you." It is clear from this verse that God intends to teach all the people of His awesome power.

The Bible itself lays down an important principle. Miracles are not intended to be a test of the truth of the things for which their testimony is summoned. The law in the Book of Deuteronomy (13:2–4) states: "If a prophet arises among you who provides a sign or a wonder, and the sign or wonder comes true, but he desires to lead you into idolatry, you shall listen to that prophet. For God is testing you to see whether you really love God with all of your heart and soul." One can conclude from reading this verse that miracles do not prove a religious truth, as they can also be performed in the cause of untruth.

Miracles have been looked upon by Bible critics in many different ways. Some have seen a pattern to the miracles. For instance, it appears that until the birth of Moses, miracles occurred for people but no individual is described as performing miracles. From Moses until Elijah, miracles are performed by individuals only for a multitude. Finally, in the period of

Elijah, the Elisha miracles are performed for individuals by individuals.

Other ways of looking at patterns of miracles relate to the purpose behind the miracle. For example, miracles of the Bible are often performed either directly by God to manifest His punitive justice against a nation (as in the cases of Sodom and Egypt), or of individuals such as Korach's death by earthquake (Numbers 17) and Uzza's instant death for touching the Ark of the Covenant (II Samuel 6:7). Miracles are sometimes performed by God to protect the Israelites, as when He furnished them with sweet water in the wilderness (Exodus 16:23). Sometimes miracles are performed by God's messenger to provide their divine calling, such as the hand of Moses which was instantly cured of its leprosy (Exodus 4:6–7).

Miracles have been called the deepest child of faith. Indeed, the biblical belief in God's omnipotence and all encompassing providence necessitates the belief in miracles at a certain stage of religious consciousness, supernatural aids in times of peril and distress. To deny the possibility of miracles appears to the believing biblical soul to be tantamount to a denial of the omnipotence of God Himself. "Is anything too wondrous for God? Is there a limit to God's power?" (Genesis 18:14; Numbers 11:23).

In the following section, we shall summarize the range of miracles that appear in the Bible. The three categories of miracles presented are those performed to manifest God's punitive justice, those demonstrating the love of God, and those demonstrating the "signs" of God.

MIRACLES DEMONSTRATING
THE WRATH OF GOD

The Flood (Genesis 7–9)

Many diverse cultures tell stories about a great flood. Since other cultures in the ancient Near East have their own stories related to an earth-wide catastrophe brought on by a deluge, scientific investigation has attempted to show that sometime near the transition between prehistory and history, flood waters from the Persian Gulf may have covered the southern section of the Mesopotamian Valley. The many common elements in all these ancient Near Eastern flood stories and those of the Bible include the ark, the raven, and the dove. However, one fundamental difference between the biblical account and the others is that in the Bible it is human sin that raised God's anger to the point where He decided to put an end to the known world (with the exception of Noah, his family, and the animals).

Clearly biblical man saw the hand of God in the flood, which was said to have lasted for 364 days, to indicate that the very cycle of nature was interrupted until heaven and earth returned to their shapes one year later. When the waters finally abated and Noah emerged from the ark, God pointed Noah to the special sign of a rainbow and stated that He would maintain a covenant with him and would never again destroy the entire world by flood. God further said: "This is the sign that I set for the covenant between Me and you. . . . I have set My rainbow in the clouds, and it shall serve as a sign of the covenant between Me and the earth" (Genesis 9:12–13).

In ancient mythology, a rainbow represented instruments

used by gods in battle. The bow would be suspended in the sky as a symbol of victory. The Hebrew word *keshet* means both "bow" and "rainbow." The biblical story of Noah clearly demonstrates that all natural events and manifestations of the divine order are invested with divine portent. For the Israelites and Jewish people today, the sign of the rainbow is an eternal reminder of God's covenant of mercy. There is even a special blessing meant to be recited upon seeing a rainbow which translates: "Praised are You, Adonai our God, Sovereign of the universe, who remembers His covenant, is faithful to it and keeps His promise."

Confusion of Tongues (Genesis 11:1–19)

The famous story of the Tower of Babel answers the questions: Where did the variety of human languages come from? and How did people disperse and populate the world? Once again, as in the Noah story, the unity of language ceased because people's rebellious actions brought the wrath of God.

According to many biblical commentators, humankind's attempt to build a brick tower to the heavens represented the tendency of people to reach too high, an attempt to displace God. Having a common language and living together encouraged their thoughts of self-aggrandizement. When God became angry enough, He put an end to the building by confounding their speech, thus scattering the people over the face of the earth (Genesis 11:7–8). The place became known as "Babel," which means "confusion."

Archaeologists have identified and uncovered a tower-like structure called a "zikurat" (literally, that which has been raised high) as being a distinctive feature of Babylonian temple complexes. It has also been confirmed that bricks were used for this enterprise. Furthermore, Cyrus Gordon in his work *Before Columbus* has corroborated the possibility of the earth's having one single language as having a historic foundation.

Destruction of Sodom and Gomorrah (Genesis 18–19)

In the well-known story of the cities of Sodom and Gomorrah (likely located on the southern end of the Dead Sea), the Bible describes God's outrage at the grave sin of the people. Although the sin is not specifically stated, many commentators seem to suggest sexual improprieties. A remarkable confrontation between Abraham and God introduced the drama, with Abraham challenging God's divine justice. Abraham pleaded with God not to destroy on the basis of his belief that some righteous people must surely exist within these two cities. When it became clear that Abraham could not find even ten righteous people, he withdrew his request.

As dawn broke, the angels of God urged Lot to quickly take his wife and daughters and leave for safety. Further, one angel said: "Flee for your life and do not look behind or stop anywhere. Flee to the hills, lest you be swept away" (Genesis 19:17). Lot was afraid to flee to the hills and identified a small town (Zoar) in close proximity to which he preferred to flee. God decided to grant his wish, and miraculously the town of Zoar was not annihilated.

The next day, God rained sulfurous fire upon the people of Sodom and Gomorrah and they were all killed. When Lot's wife turned back to look, she was transformed into a pillar of salt.

To this day, there are some salt-encrusted rock formations in the Dead Sea area that suggest the figure of Lot's wife!

The Ten Plagues (Exodus 7:14–12:34)

As a result of the affliction suffered by the Israelites while enslaved in Egypt, God brings terror upon the Egyptians by means of ten plagues: seven which were brought on by Moses or Aaron raising his staff and three sent directly by God. The plagues included turning the Nile to blood, infestation of frogs, lice affecting both humans and beasts, flies, murrain affecting the cattle, boils, heavy hail, locusts devouring the crops, three days of darkness, and the death of the firstborn, both human and beast. This episode features prominently in the Passover Seder service.

The straightforward meaning of the biblical text of the ten plagues appears to be that God brought extraordinary events which were designed to save the Israelites from their fate. In doing so, God interfered with the ordinary processes of nature. This intervention is often described as a "miracle." The story of the plagues, however, uses two terms for the extraordinary acts of God—*ot*, meaning a "sign," and *mofet*, meaning a "marvel" or "wonder." Their use implies divine action as well as a natural world whose laws are flexible and subject to personal forces.

There are a variety of opinions and interpretations regarding the ten plagues and their historicity. Some commentators considered them legendary and interpretive, and that the real thrust of the story was the release of the Israelite people by God who chose them for a special mission. Other medieval interpreters assumed that these so-called wonders only appeared as divine interventions, but had in fact been built into the process of creation from its inception. Still others, such as the philosopher Thomas Aquinas, were of the opinion that any miracle was an event that cannot be explained.

The lengthy biblical story of the ten plagues has fascinated scientists who have tried to find various scientific explanations for the disasters visited upon Egypt. Many have come up with what has come to be known as the domino theory of causes—from the red algae that turned the waters to "blood" to the bacteria-ridden flies that caused boils, and the moldy grain so lethal that it could have killed the firstborn of Egypt within hours. The plague of hail is more difficult to account for since such weather is rare in Egypt. As for the plague of darkness, perhaps it was a sandstorm. The siroccos of Egypt whip up dust clouds for days at a time, and these clouds have the capacity to shade the entire land in twilight.

The Bible says this extraordinary death and destruction was God's work but clearly the ancient story of miracle after miracle remains a mystery difficult for any person to fully explain.

Today, however, one understands the nature of the ten plagues; clearly their place in history has been firmly established. The allusion to them, the Song of the Sea (Exodus 15), and the repeated references to God as the Redeemer of the Israelites from Egyptian bondage, all of which have been included in the daily liturgy, clearly point to the fact that rabbinic thinkers wanted God to be thanked and worshiped for His amazing redemptive powers.

Death of Nadav and Avihu (Leviticus 10:1)

In the opening sentences of the tenth chapter of the Book of Leviticus the reader is startled to learn of the great calamity that happened to the tabernacle. There, the two sons of Aaron, the most promising young men in the camp of Israel, were struck down by sudden death for bringing strange fires into the house of God. The story is both miraculous and mysterious. It is told with such brevity that the details that arouse our curiosity are omitted. What was that strange fire that these two sons offered before God? Why was God's wrath so great that the two were punished for what seemed to be intense devotion and enthusiasm? Many rabbinic explanations have been offered. One explanation stated that the sons perished because they presumed to decide a question of law in the presence of Moses their teacher. A second explanation put forward that the two sons were intoxicated. A third explanation was that they entered the sanctuary without having previously washed their hands.

The rabbis went on to explain that mysteriously only the souls of the two sons were consumed, their bodies remaining untouched. It is unlikely that we will ever know the real reason for God's anger and their punishment. One thing is certain, God has the extraordinary power to change a person's fate and He is prepared to use that power when necessary.

People at Taberah Consumed by Fire (Numbers 11:1)

In this famous biblical scene the Israelites complained bitterly before God. God heard their crying and was so angered that He caused a fire to break out which ravaged the outskirts of the camp. When the people then appealed to God, Moses prayed and God caused the fire to die down. The name of the place became known as Taberah (i.e., burning), because a fire burned in the midst of the people.

Death of Korach, Dathan, and Abihu by Earthquake
(Numbers 16:31)

Some of the Israelites began to be discontented with Moses' leadership. Dathan and Abihu from the tribe of Reuben were two of the aggrieved. Korach, the Levite, was aggrieved with Aaron, to whose family all priestly privilege had been confined. These two groups of malcontents worked separately, and in the end they were cut off by different extraordinary acts of God. As the story unfolded, Moses said that all will know God has sent him if these men die a death not common to most people. However, if the ground opens up and swallows them alive into the pit, then all will understand these rebels despised God. The earth indeed opened up and swallowed them as well as all of the followers of Korach. Fire came from God and devoured the two hundred and fifty men who offered the incense.

There were numerous rebellions in the wilderness, directed against either God or His emissary. In each case the rebels were reported to have died of a plague, fire, or in battle. Only twice, when the position of Moses was severely attacked, was there extraordinary unusual punishment: by leprosy, when Miriam and Aaron challenged their brother Moses (Numbers 12) and by earthquake in the story of Korach and his men. In the people's uprisings against God, the consequences did not lie outside the human realm but in the challenges to Moses, the punishments were supernatural.

The intent of the biblical tradition of rebellion seems to be that a rebellion against the priestly leaders was a rebellion against God. Those who objected to the leaders were exposed to divine wrath, which was extraordinarily severe, when God's authority was challenged indirectly through His chosen leaders.

Over the course of time the story of Korach assumed great importance. The rabbis of the Talmud often viewed themselves as direct spiritual descendants of Moses and interpreted Korach's challenge to Moses as a warning to their own contemporaries who challenged the divine sanctity of human teaching. However, since a repetition of biblical miracles such as the earthquake could not be counted on, the rabbis often threatened their challenges with loss of eternal life and a place in the world-to-come.

Destruction of Jericho (Joshua 6:6)

The sixth chapter of the Book of Joshua describes the capture of the city of Jericho. Here is some of the exciting narrative from the Bible:

> God said to Joshua: "Behold, I will deliver Jericho and her king and warriors into your hands. Let all of the troops march around the city and complete one circuit of the city. Do this for six days, with seven priests carrying seven ram's horns preceding the Ark. On the seventh day, march around the city seven times, with the priests blowing the horns. And when a long blast is heard on the horn, as soon as you hear the sound of the horn, all the people will give a loud shout. Then, the city wall will collapse and the people shall advance. . . . (Joshua 6:1–6)

In verse 20 of chapter 6 we learn that the walls of Jericho collapsed when the horns were blown and the voices of the people were raised.

Jericho was one of the first formidable military challenges of Joshua's regime. Because of its high walls, Jericho could not be captured by a massive onslaught. Because it had ample food, it could not be forced into submission by a lengthy siege.

There have been several scientific interpretations for the collapse of the walls. Some researchers have pointed to the possibility of an earthquake. Jericho lies in the Jordan Rift Valley, some 840 feet below sea level. In this region the earth's crust is known to be fairly unstable and quakes are quite common. However, one might ask, what is the chance of a huge quake occurring on the final day of the siege?

Some scholars have suggested that the collapse was some-
how caused by the sounds of the rams horns and the shouting
of the soldiers. Although high frequencies have been known
to shatter glass, it would be rather unlikely that the shouts of
many people and the shrill tones of the horns would be able
to move walls of stone.

Archaeologists have uncovered the foundations of the walls
of Jericho which were 12 to 14 feet wide and a tower 30 feet
high. Walls were built from stones with flat surfaces made by
chipping them so that they fitted well on top of each other.
Because of the effort and time required, the stones were not
very carefully prepared. Some have hypothesized that the
materials used to construct the Jericho walls were mud bricks,
and that, as the defenders stood on top of them, they began to
crack and slowly erode. On the last day of the siege when
there were likely more people on the walls than on previous
days, one of the walls apparently collapsed.

These are several of the theories put forth by those who
have attempted to understand the collapse of the Jericho walls
more in scientific terms and less as an extraordinary act of
God.

Slaying of the Philistines (I Samuel 5:11)

When the Philistines captured the Ark of God, they brought
it to Ashdod and placed it in the temple of the Dagon, the
national god of the Philistines. Early the next day, they found
Dagon lying face down on the ground in front of the Ark of
God. They picked up Dagon and put it back into place, only
to have it lying prone on the ground in front of the Ark of
God the very next day. This time its head and hands were cut
off.

It was then that the hand of God brought havoc upon Ashdod and its territory, striking it with hemorrhoids. The people of Ashdod realized that God's hand caused this extraordinarily cruel plague and sent messengers to have the Ark of God moved to Gath. There, too, God caused great panic and struck the people with hemorrhoids. From there the Ark was moved to Ekron where again the people were stricken with hemorrhoids.

We see the extraordinary power of God's wrath and His ability to wreak havoc upon the Philistines. The burden of this passage is the mysterious and miraculous power of the Ark, bringing destruction to the Philistines.

The Slaying of Uzzah (II Samuel 6:7)

In this story King David assembled the Israelites and the troops set out to bring the Ark of God into Jerusalem. There was much singing and dancing in honor of this auspicious occasion. It was then that Uzzah reached out for the Ark of God and grasped it, for the oxen had stumbled. God was incensed with him and struck him down on the spot, and Uzzah died. It is not really known why Uzzah was slain. It appears that his punishment was due to his irreverence toward the Ark. Rashi, the medieval commentator, commented that it was presumptuous of Uzzah to have assumed that the Ark required his assistance. In any event, the wrath of God brought Uzzah's life to an extraordinary sudden end.

The Withering of Jeroboam's Hand (I Kings 13:4)

A prophetic warning is given to Jeroboam accompanied by a miraculous occurrence. Here is how the Bible tells it:

There came a man of God out of Judah by the word of God to Beth El. And Jeroboam was standing by the altar to offer. And he cried against the altar by the word of God, and said: "O altar, altar, thus says God: Behold, a son shall be born to the house of David, Josiah by name. And upon you shall he sacrifice the priests of the high places that offer upon you, and men's bones shall they burn upon you." And he gave a sign the same day saying: "This is the sign which God has spoken: Behold the altar shall be rent, and the ashes that are upon it shall be poured out." And it came to pass when the king heard the saying of the man of God, that Jeroboam put forth his hand from the altar, saying: "Lay hold on him." And his hand, which he put forth against him, stiffened so that he could not draw it back to him. The altar also was rent, and the ashes poured out from the altar, according to the sign which the man of God had given by the word of God. And the king answered and said to the man of God: "Entreat now the favor of God, and pray for me, that my hand be restored to me." And the man of God prayed to God and the king's hand was restored to him, and became as it was before. (I Kings 13:1–10)

Uzziah Smitten with Leprosy (II Chronicles 26:13)

Uzziah became King when he was the tender age of sixteen. Early in his career he did everything to please God, and God made him prosper. He breached the walls of Gath and Ashdod, built towns, built towers in Jerusalem, and had a huge army of well-trained warriors. Soon his fame began to spread over all the land.

His fame led to arrogance, and he began to act corruptly. He trespassed against God by entering the Temple to offer incense on the incense altar. Subsequently he was asked by the priest Azariah to leave, since it was not Uzziah's right to be in such a consecrated place. Uzziah, holding the censer and ready to burn incense, became angry, and in front of the priests, leprosy broke out on his forehead. For the remainder of his life, King Uzziah lived in isolated quarters as a leper.

Once again we see the wrath of God when Uzziah is struck with leprosy, the most dreaded of all biblical diseases.

MIRACLES DEMONSTRATING THE LOVE OF GOD

Just as God brought about miracles as a result of His wrath and anger, so too God showed Himself by working wonders as a result of His love. The following is a cross section of miracles in the Bible that were brought about by God as a result of His love.

The Crossing of the Red Sea (Exodus 14:21)

The spectacular fleeing of the Israelites from the pursuing Egyptians forms the conclusion of the tale of liberation. After four hundred years of Egyptian slavery, the Egyptian Pharaoh released the Israelites after God's plague of slaying the firstborn sons appeared to break his will. After the Israelites hastily made their exit, Pharaoh's chariots were in hot pursuit. Soon it became obvious that the Sea of Reeds stood in the way of freedom for the Israelites. It was then that God said to Moses: "Lift up your rod and stretch out your hand over the sea and divide it. And the children of Israel shall go into the midst of the sea on dry ground" (Exodus 14:16).

Moses followed God's command. A fierce wind parted the sea and the Israelites were able to cross safely. Clearly this was the greatest of all miraculous events to occur in the Bible. The entire people of Israel were saved!

The sea mentioned in the biblical account has generally been assumed to be the Reed Sea, which may have been an extensive bay of either the Mediterranean or the Red Sea. Some have said that the area is more likely to be the Bitter Lakes in the center of the lowlands, now occupied by the Suez Canal. The Bitter Lakes were given their name because of the high percentage of alkali salts in the water, which in certain parts was very shallow. Scientists have said that it is quite possible that a strong wind pushed these waters toward one end of the lake, thus lowering the level at the other end. Since the exodus began in the spring (at Passover time), this is the season known for powerful winds in the region. If the Israelites crossed and the wind changed direction, the water could have returned to its usual level and the Egyptian army may have become bogged down in the muddy waters.

A relatively new interpretation of historical documents by a professor at Johns Hopkins University puts the exodus of the Israelites from Egypt about two hundred years earlier than had been previously assumed. Dr. Hans Geotaxy links the parting of the waves that swallowed the pursuing Egyptians to a powerful tidal wave generated by the same volcanic eruption that apparently wiped out the Minoan civilization. This new estimate is that the exodus occurred in 1477 B.C.E. If this revised date is correct, it is possible to account for the waters that drowned the Egyptians as the consequence of the tidal wave, an established natural phenomenon, rather than as the result of divine intervention. Other scholars suggest that the parting of the waves should be viewed as mythology without attempting to find a naturalistic explanation.

However, no examination of presumed natural causes should overshadow the central fact: Israel experienced the event as divinely determined, a miracle in the true sense. It was God who brought about the Egyptians' downfall. The Israelites saw the wondrous power of God and had faith in His power and justice.

The Song of the Sea (Exodus 15) has become a part of the Jewish prayer liturgy, inserted into the morning daily service. Clearly this was done so worshipers are reminded on a daily basis of the miraculous exodus from Egypt and God's omnipotence and concern for His people.

Sweetening the Waters of Marah (Exodus 15:23–25)

Here is the complete quotation from the Bible regarding the bitter water in the desert.

> And they came to Marah but they could not drink the waters of Marah for they were bitter. The people grumbled against Moses, saying, "What shall we drink?" So he cried out to God, and God showed him a piece of wood. He threw it into the water and the water became sweet.

This is certainly one of the great miracles in the Bible. Yet it has been suggested that there are scientific bases for this and similar procedures, which are known among people in various continents. For example, it is a fact that wood from an oak tree contains the chemical tannin which neutralizes albuminous matter, coagulates it, and causes it to sink to the bottom. The biblical text appears to limit God's participation in this case to showing Moses a way to sweeten the water, without suggesting that the process itself is miraculous. The Itture Torah commentary (volume 8, pg. 129) does not understand the "bitter waters" in a literal sense. Rather, it comments that bitterness was not the actual condition of the water, but rather

the Israelites felt bitter and therefore, whatever they tasted
was bitter to them.

Manna Sent from Heaven (Exodus 16:14)

About six weeks after the Israelites left Egypt, when they were
not yet accustomed to life in the wilderness, the provisions
which they had brought with them were exhausted. Soon after
there appeared on the face of the wilderness a fine, scale-like
thing, fine as the hoarfrost on the ground. On seeing it, the
Israelites asked one another: What is this? (in Hebrew, "man
hoo"). They did not know what it was, but Moses explained to
them that it was bread that God had given them to eat. It was
like coriander seed, white, and had the taste of wafers made
with honey.

The manna was miraculously supplied to the Israelites until
they entered Canaan and the fruit of the land was available
(Joshua 5:12). According to talmudic tradition, many miracles
occurred in connection with the daily descent of manna. No
one could keep it for the next day or possess more than one
omer, for it bred worms. Yet, the Sabbath portion, which came
down in a double portion on Friday, remained fresh for the
sacred day.

The commentator Bachya states if what was gathered of the
manna amounted in any case to one *omer*, why should everyone be urged to collect "as much of it as each of you requires
to eat" (Exodus 16:16)? Surely a little amount of it would have
been more than sufficient. Bachya answers that the Bible
intended to teach us that people must do for themselves what
is necessary and not rely on miracles.

Many botanists state that it has long been known that the
extraordinary food the Israelites consumed in the wilderness
for forty years which they called manna has a biological

counterpart that exists naturally in the Sinai Peninsula. The substance was in the past believed to be an exudation of the tamarisk, but it is now known to originate in an excretion of two scaled-insects that live in symbiosis with the tamarisk.

According to Bodenheimer in *Biblical Archaeologist*, 10, 1947 (pp. 2–6), a chemical analysis of the excretions has revealed that they contain a mixture of three basic sugars with pectin. The plant saps on which these insects feed are rich in carbohydrates but extremely poor in nitrogen. To acquire a minimum amount of nitrogen for their metabolism, they must consume great quantities of sap. The excess passes from them in honeydew excretions which quickly change in the dry air of the desert into sticky solid drops.

Today the Bedouin tribes view manna as a great delicacy, harvesting it in June and July.

There are several major differences between the natural manna and the manna described in the Book of Exodus. The manna of today is relatively sparse and could not possibly provide enough food for the entire people of Israel. It is, of course, found on the Sabbath as well as on other days of the week. The biblical manna is clearly meant to be a food brought from heaven by God, interrupting the natural order by willing it so. It is meant to show God's care, concern, and love for His people. That is why manna has come to be known as "heavenly food," as it states in Psalm 105:40: "God satisfied them with food from heaven."

Water Drawn from the Rock (Exodus 17:5 and Numbers 20:7)

Realizing after they had encamped at Rephidim that there was no water to drink, the Israelites began to quarrel with Moses, asking him to provide them with water. Moses, hearing their complaints, feared for his life and called to God for assistance and divine intervention. God spoke these words to Moses: "Pass before the people and take with you some of the elders of Israel, and take along the rod with which you struck the Nile, and set out. I will be standing there before you on the rock at Horeb. Strike the rock and water will issue forth from it, and the people will drink" (Exodus 17:5–6). Moses hit the rock and the people were able to drink.

In a later story appearing in the Book of Numbers, Moses was again told that he and Aaron are to take the rod, assemble the community, and order the rock to deliver its water. At the earlier incident Moses had been commanded to strike the rock physically. Here, he was ordered to command the rock verbally to spew forth its water. (No reason was given for the difference in commands.) Instead, Moses struck the rod twice with his rod, and the Israelites were given water. According to this explanation, the miracle was to have rested in the power of the words spoken to the inanimate stone in God's name. Instead, Moses performed a physical act, revealing his lack of trust in God's word. As a result, Moses and Aaron learned that they would not lead the Israelites directly into the Holy Land.

The commentator Maimonides (introduction to *Ethics of the Fathers* 4) stresses the apparent anger of Moses, who is quoted in the Bible as saying "listen you rebels." The commentator Ibn Ezra thus sees the punishment of Moses as his inability as a leader to control his emotions and anger.

The Alcott Chemin notes that Moses and Aaron said: "Shall we get water for you out of this rock?" thereby emphasizing their own roles rather than God's role in the miracle.

To this day modern thinkers find it difficult to understand why Moses' transgression left him with a punishment which does not seem to fit the crime.

It is interesting that Christian Scriptures have preserved an ancient Jewish legend of a rock containing water that followed the Israelites throughout their trek in the desert (Targum Jonathan on Numbers 21:19). They compare the rock of Meribah to Jesus himself.

In terms of natural causes, geologists have identified two common types of groundwater. One is called fossil water, accumulated centuries ago when the climate was much more humid than today. In most cases, fossil water, because of its long contact with the rocks, is high in mineral content, making it bitter and in many instances undrinkable.

However, most of the water found in the ground originates as rain, which trickles through the soil into bedrock where it moves through crevices. The downward flow is stopped when the water encounters permeable rocks. Under the force of gravity, it continues to flow more or less horizontally through the rock formation that is referred to as the reservoir rock. In some places, the reservoir rock is exposed—as on the side of a canyon—and one may find springs. In these places, the water seeps out of the reservoir and flows down the slope. These are the locations of oases.

In places where the reservoir rock is close to the surface, the water can be withdrawn by either a pump or more primitively by lowering a bucket through a vertical shaft which has been dug through the rocks overlying the water table.

These desert holes are quite common in a few desert regions. There is scientific opinion that some of the old water holes in the Sinai Desert which yield water today were used by the Israelites. In fact, during the Yom Kippur War of 1973, when the Israeli army had a large Egyptian force surrounded, the Egyptian soldiers obtained water from the so-called Wells of Moses, a series of water holes in the western Sinai.

The Serpent of Brass Heals (Numbers 21:9)

In a most astounding story presented in Numbers 21, the Israelites spoke out against God and against Moses, complaining of the miserable food in the wilderness. God sent fiery serpents among the people, who were bitten by them and died. It was then that the Israelites appealed to Moses, having realized their sin of speaking against God. Moses interceded. Here is the way the Bible tells the rest of the story:

> Then God said to Moses, "Make a fiery figure and mount it on a standard. And if anyone who is bitten looks at it, that person shall recover." Moses made a copper serpent and mounted it on a standard. And when anyone was bitten by a serpent, he would look at the copper serpent and recover.

There are numerous tales of the healing influence of serpents in many cultural traditions. Interestingly, the medical symbol commonly used today features two serpents. There is no question, however, that the tale of the mounted copper serpent which had a therapeutic effect during the plague of fiery snakes raises many questions. For instance, the very creation of such an object seems to contradict the second of the Ten Commandments which forbids the making of images.

The question of the healing serpents was again raised in the apocryphal book *Wisdom of Solomon* (16:5–7) which says that the serpent served both as a lesson and a symbol: "The person who turned toward it was saved, not by what one saw but by God, the Savior of all." The Mishneh (Rosh HaShanah 318) teaches the following: "Could the serpent kill or keep alive? Rather it is to teach you that when the Israelites directed their thoughts toward God in heaven, they were healed. Otherwise, they perished."

The brazen serpent made by Moses was naturally preserved as an object of adoration by the Israelites. When in later centuries it appeared to become an object of idolatrous worship, it was destroyed by King Hezekiah (II Kings 18:4).

Passage of the Jordan (Joshua 3:14)

Chapter 3 of the Book of Joshua presents the reader with the miraculous parting of the Jordan River. Here is the narrative in the Bible's words:

> Joshua rose up early in the morning and they left Shittim and came to the Jordan, he and all the children of Israel. They lodged there before they passed over. After three days, the officers went through the midst of the camp. They commanded the people: "When you see the ark of the covenant of the Lord your God, and the priests the Levites bearing it, then you shall leave your place and go after it. Yet there shall be a space between you and it, about two thousand cubits by measure. Do not come near to it, that you may know the way by which you must go. For you have not passed this way heretofore." And Joshua said to the people: "Sanctify yourselves, for tomorrow God will do wonders among you." And Joshua spoke to the priests, saying: "Take up the ark of the covenant, and pass on before the people." And they took up the ark of the covenant and went before the people. And God said to Joshua, "This day I will begin to magnify you in the sight of all Israel, that you may know that as I was with Moses, so I will be with you. And you shall command the priests that bear the ark of the covenant saying, 'When you come to the brink of the waters of the Jordan, you shall stand still in the Jordan.'"
>
> And Joshua said to the children of Israel: "Come here, and listen to the words of God. . . ." Behold, the ark of the

covenant of God of all the earth passes on before you over the
Jordan. Now therefore, take twelve men of the tribes of Israel,
for every tribe a man. And it shall come to pass, when the
soles of the priests that bear the ark of God of all the earth
shall rest in the waters of the Jordan, that the waters of the
Jordan shall be cut off, even the waters that come down from
above, and they shall stand in one heap." And it came to pass
when the people left their tents to pass over the Jordan that
the priests, bearing the ark of the covenant were before the
people. When they that bore the ark were come to the Jordan
and the feet of the priests that bore the ark were dipped in the
brink of the water that the waters which came down from
above stood, and rose up in one heap . . . and the people
passed over right against Jericho. And the priests that bore the
ark of the covenant of God stood firm on dry ground in the
midst of the Jordan, while all of Israel passed over on dry
ground, until all the nation were passed clean over the Jordan.
(Joshua 3:1–17)

In the Bible, the Jordan River is associated in particular
with Jericho and is frequently mentioned with that city near
which the Israelites crossed the Jordan. In biblical times, the
Jordan was crossed by means of its fords. Jacob is described in
Genesis 32:10 as passing over the Jordan with a staff on his
way from Beth El. There is no doubt that the most famous
passage of the Jordan was that of the Israelites opposite
Jericho, as previously related. As it was very difficult to ford
the river at that place during that season, the sudden cessation
of the flow of the river was regarded as miraculous. Psalm
114:3ff describes the crossing of the Jordan as one of God's
greatest miracles when it stated that "the Jordan ran back-
ward." The *Encyclopedia Judaica* states that several times in
history it has been recorded that the Jordan ceased flowing: in
1267 it stopped flowing for eight hours, in 1546 it ceased

flowing for two whole days, and in 1927 for 21.5 hours. In all three cases the cessation was the result of earthquakes which caused the high banks to collapse, blocking the river bed and stopping its flow.

A solid testimony of a miracle's occurrence is a tangible object taken from the site of the event. In the story of Joshua and the people crossing the Jordan River, Joshua commanded them, at the time of the crossing, to take twelve stones from the Jordan "that this may be a sign among you when your children ask in time to come saying, 'What do these stones mean to you?'" (Joshua 4:6). Similarly, Moses, in the name of God, commands the people to put some of the heavenly manna into a vessel to keep as a remembrance (Exodus 16:32–34).

Daniel's Miracles:
a. The Furnace Rendered Harmless (Daniel 3:20)

The biblical book of Daniel, consisting of 12 chapters, is made up of two parts. The first six chapters, with its own version of a burning bush motif, tell of the miraculous deliverance of Daniel and his three friends who were exiled to Babylon by Nebuchadnezzar before the fall of Judea. These three high-ranking administrators were greatly affected by the decree which King Nebuchadnezzar issued to all the top functionaries, namely to bow down to the image which he had set up. The three ignored the decree, and the king ordered Shadrach, Mishach, and Abednego thrown into a blazing furnace. But not even their clothes were singed. King Nebuchadnezzar was obviously so moved by the miracle that he had witnessed before his very eyes that he offered a blessing to God: "Blessed be the God of Shadrach, Meshach, and Abednego, who sent His angel to save His servants who, trusting in Him, flouted the king's decree at the risk of their own lives rather than worship any god but their own God."

He further set forth an order that anyone who blasphemed the God of Shadrach, Meshach, and Abednego shall be torn limb from limb, for there is no God who is able to save in this way. It is then that King Nebuchadnezzar said these concluding words of chapter 3 of the Book of Daniel: "The signs and wonders that the Most High God has worked for me I am pleased to tell. How great are God's signs and how mighty God's wonders. God's kingdom is an everlasting one and God's dominion endures through all generations."

It appears that the purpose of the story of the furnace rendered harmless is an attempt to teach the people that the God of Israel is the only God and that in faithfulness to His worship one must be ready to suffer martyrdom if necessary. The narrative is also a powerful polemic against idolatry.

b. Daniel Unhurt by the Lions (Daniel 6:16)

In the sixth chapter of the Book of Daniel, Daniel is accused by his rivals of showing disregard for the Persian King Darius. The King had no choice but to sentence him to death. Daniel was cast into a den of lions. Here is the way the Bible describes the rest of the story:

> The king spoke and said to Daniel: "Your God whom you serve continually, He will deliver you." A stone was brought and laid upon the mouth of the den, and the king sealed it with his own signet. . . . Then the king went to his palace, and passed the night fasting; neither were diversions brought before him, and his sleep fled from him. Then the king arose very early in the morning, and went in quickly to the den of lions. And when he came near to the den to Daniel, he cried

with a pained voice; the king spoke and said to Daniel, "O Daniel, servant of the living God, is your God, whom you serve continually, able to deliver you from the lions?" Then Daniel said to the king: "O king, live forever! My God has sent His angel and has shut the lions' mouths, and they have not hurt me. (Daniel 6:17–23)

At the conclusion of this chapter, King Darius decreed that God is the living God, steadfast forever, and that God's kingdom and dominion are eternal. God rescues and works signs and wonders, both in heaven and earth.

In this story, King Darius expressed his profound belief in the power of Daniel's God to rescue His faithful follower. The king appeared as a true friend of Daniel throughout the chapter, and here as a believer in God. It seems that the miraculous saving power of God's angel is intended to teach a lesson not to the king, but to his heathen subjects.

It is said that this story happened toward the end of the biblical period, about the year 170 B.C.E. This was the time that the Jewish people were under the oppressive rule of the Syrian-Greeks, who threatened their religion's very survival. Certainly the reassurance of God's angel as Daniel's rescuer must have raised the national morale of the Jewish people.

Jonah Survives the Whale (The Book of Jonah)

The miraculous tale of Jonah, who lived about 750 B.C.E., is well known. Ordered by God to prophesy the destruction of Nineveh for its wickedness, Jonah attempted to escape from the divine command by sailing from the land of Israel. A tremendous storm severely affected the sailing of the ship. The sailors, either out of reverence for a man of God or because they believed Jonah was the cause of the storm, appealed to him for guidance. As tensions continued to mount, Jonah was cast into the sea, and the sea ceased raging. It was then that God prepared a large fish that swallowed Jonah, who remained in its belly for three days and nights. Jonah prayed to God and several days later the large fish ejected Jonah onto dry land. Jonah received a second bidding from God and this time obeyed it unquestioningly. The people of Ninevah accepted the warning, repented sincerely, and were forgiven.

Many of the main motifs of this book are similar to those found in the literature of other cultures. There are many stories about a person's being swallowed by a great fish and rescued thereafter, including those of Heracles, the Hesione, and Perseus and Andromeda. However, only in the Book of Jonah is the man in the fish rescued not by a force such as fire or sword but by prayer. Basically the same situation in the Book of Jonah is found in the previous story of Daniel's rescue from the lions' den and the salvation of Daniel's three friends from the fiery furnace. In all these stories, the motif of swallowing becomes a symbol for the act of faith between God and humans.

The majority of modern biblical scholars consider the Book of Jonah to be either a parable or an allegory. As a parable, the Book of Jonah would be an attempt to teach great lessons by means of an imaginative story. These lessons would include that God accepts true repentance and that gentiles should not be begrudged God's love and forgiveness.

According to the allegorical interpretation, Jonah is representative of Israel. His disappearance into the sea in the fish symbolizes his own isolation from people, God, and exile from the world. His ejection upon dry land symbolizes the restoration. Like Jonah, Israel flees from the duty which God has laid upon it, and like him, Israel exhibits ill will believing that God has any fate for the heathen except destruction.

Miracle Biblical Pregnancies

There are a host of women in the Bible who are described as barren, not having the ability to bear children. The Israelites have always been a people of the family, and the inability to have children was a difficult situation for any family to bear. The following is a summary of miraculous pregnancies which occurred due to prayer and divine intervention.

a. God closed all the wombs of Avimelech's household because Avimelech had taken Sarah for himself. After Sarah was restored to Abraham, Abraham prayed and the women bore children (Genesis 20:17–18).

b. Although Sarah was old and unable to bear children before, she gave birth to Isaac when she was 90 years old, as God fulfilled His promise. Abraham was 100 years old when Isaac was born (Genesis 21:1–5).

c. Rebekkah was barren until her husband Isaac prayed for her. Then she conceived and gave birth to twins—Jacob and Esau (Genesis 25:21–26).

d. God opened the womb of the barren Rachel, and she gave birth to Joseph and Benjamin (Genesis 30:22–24).

e. The angel of God appeared to Manoah's barren wife, foretelling that she would bear a son (Samson) who would begin to deliver Israel from the Philistines (Judges 13:3, 5).

f. God shut up Hannah's womb so that she was childless. But then, in answer to Hannah's intense prayer, she gave birth to Samuel (Samuel 1:1–20).

g. Although her husband was "too old," the Shunammite woman bore a son, thus fulfilling Elisha's word (II Kings 4:13–17).

BIBLICAL MIRACLE
STORIES OF ELIJAH AND ELISHA

The prophet Elijah, who lived in the ninth century before the common era during the reign of Ahab, King of Israel, has been described as the most romantic and enigmatic character in the whole range of Jewish history. He was perhaps the leading miracle man in all Jewish folklore and has been credited with countless miraculous deeds. When Ahab, influenced by his wife Jezebel of Tyre, had given himself to the worship of the Phoenician god Baal, Elijah's emergence was sudden and dramatic. He appeared before the scene and predicted a drought as penalty for the introduction of the Phoenician cult into Israel. Then followed a wondrous scene at Mount Carmel, demonstrating the supreme power of God and the impotence of Baal. Baal's prophets, who proved to be imposters, were slain at Elijah's bidding. Due to Elijah's great zeal for God, the Bible tells us that the prophet was transported up to heaven in a whirlwind without dying (II Kings 2:6–12). It became a cherished widespread belief that the prophet Elijah, who had never died, would appear again to restore Israel. "And he will turn the hearts of fathers to their children and the hearts of children to their fathers" (Malachi 4:6).

As the ever-ready defending champion of his people, Elijah is supposed to roam the earth testing the hospitality and goodness of men and women. As the "angel of the covenant" (Malachi 3:1) and protector of children, he is believed to be the invisible participant at circumcisions. Seated at the right hand of the *sandek,* the person privileged to hold the child during the circumcision ceremony, invisible Elijah guards the infant from danger. The symbolic chair known as "Elijah's chair," set aside for the prophet, is left in position for three days, the dangerous period following the operation.

According to tradition, Elijah will settle every doubtful case in Judaism shortly before the advent of the Messiah. Elijah's cup of wine, which is placed on the Passover Seder table, is linked with a talmudic dispute as to whether four or five glasses of wine are to be used at the Seder celebration. Hence the extra cup, known as Elijah's cup, conveys that the question could not be solved by the authorities of the Talmud and must therefore wait for Elijah's decision.

Elisha, another prophet and contemporary of Elijah, flourished during and after the reign of King Jehoram. The biblical stories reflect the esteem with which he was held by the people. Numerous miracles were attributed to him, including the resurrection of the dead. His chief importance is that he was the disciple and successor of Elijah, and like Elijah, is depicted as not only kind and generous but brave and forceful.

Biblical Miracle Stories of Elijah

Elijah and the Widow (I Kings 17)

In this chapter from the Book of Kings, Elijah makes his initial appearance on the scene. He comes onto the scene with great suddenness and like Moses, nothing is told of his earlier life. His stories abound in miracle and marvel which clearly portray God's omnipotent power.

There was a drought in Israel, and the word of God came to Elijah as follows:

"Arise, go to Zarephat, which belongs to Zidon, and dwell there. Behold, I have commanded a widow who lives there to sustain you." So he arose and went to Zarephat, and when he came to the city gate, a widow was there gathering sticks. He called to her and said: "Fetch me, I pray you, a little water in a vessel, that I may drink." And as she was going to bring it, he called to her and said: "Bring me I pray you a morsel of bread in your hand." And she said: "As the Lord your God lives, I do not have any cake, only a handful of meal in the jar, and a little oil in the cruse, and behold, I am gathering two sticks, that I may go in and dress it for me and my son, that we may eat it, and die." And Elijah said to her: "Do not be afraid. Go and do as you have said, but make me a little cake first, and bring it to me, and afterward make for you and for your son." For thus says the God of Israel: "The jar of meal shall be spent, neither shall the cruse of oil fail, until the day that God sends rain upon the land." And she went and did according to the saying of Elijah, and she, and he, and her house, did eat many days, neither did the oil fail, according to the word of God, which God spoke to Elijah. (I Kings 17:9–16)

Were the miraculous feeding of the widow amazing in and of itself, one additional miracle can be detailed. The widow's son fell ill and eventually died. The widow bitterly protested against Elijah coming to her house, which, in her opinion, was the cause of her son's death. Elijah took the child and carried him into his own bed and lay with him. He cried to God while stretching himself upon the child, appealing to God to let the child's soul return. God heard Elijah's voice, the soul of the child returned, and the child was revived. Seeing her child miraculously return to life, the woman said to Elijah: "Now I know that you are a man of God, and that the word of God in your mouth is the truth." The wondrous return of her son's life resulted in a full and explicit avowal of faith in God by the widow.

Ahaziah's Troops Consumed by Fire (II Kings 1:10)

The opening chapter of the Second Book of Kings describes the revolt of Moab against Israel. King Ahaziah suffered injury from a fall and sent his messengers to inquire of Baal-zebub, the Philistine god, whether or not he would recover. At that moment an angel of God appeared, telling Elijah to inform the king's messengers that he would die. Here is the amazing conclusion to the story as told in the Book of Kings 1:9–13; 15–17:

> Then the king sent to him a captain of fifty with his fifty. And he went up to him, and behold, he sat on the top of the hill. And he spoke to him: "O man of God, the king has said: 'Come down.'" And Elijah answered and said to the captain of fifty: "If I be a man of God, let fire come down from heaven and consume you and your fifty." And again he sent to him another captain of fifty with his fifty. And he answered and said to him: "O man of God, thus has the king said: Come down quickly." And Elijah answered and said to them: "If I be a man of God, let fire come down from heaven and consume you and your fifty." And the fire of God came down from heaven and consumed him and his fifty. . . . And the angel of God said to Elijah: "Go down with him and do not be afraid of him." And he arose, and went down with him to the king. And he said to him: "Thus says God: Forasmuch as you have sent messengers to inquire of Baal-zebub the god of Ekron, is it because there is no God in Israel to inquire of His word? Therefore you shall not come down from the bed from which you have gone up, but shall surely die." So he died according to the word of God which Elijah had spoken.

Once again the wrath of God for Ahaziah's impiety brought about the miraculous fires that consumed him and his army.

Elijah Obtains Rain (I Kings 18:41)

In the time of King Ahab, the Israelites were wavering between God and Baal. Ahab was a generous ruler but weak-willed and dominated by his Phoenician wife. It was high treason to proclaim the God of Israel, and once again the figure of Elijah stands out in greatness. At the end of chapter 18 of the First Book of Kings, a drought has settled upon the land. Here is how the Bible tells the story:

> Elijah went up to the top of Carmel, and bowed himself down upon the earth, putting his face between his knees. And he said to his servant: "Go up now, look toward the sea." And he went up, and looked, and said; "There is nothing." And he said: "Go again seven times." And it came to pass at the seventh time, that he said: "Behold, there arises a cloud out of the sea, as small as a man's hand." And he said: "Go up, say to Ahav: 'Make ready your chariot, and get down, that the rain does not stop you.'" And it happened in a short while that the heaven grew black with clouds and wind, and there was a great rain. (II Kings 18:42–45)

There are many miracle stories related to bringing rain in time of drought, especially in rabbinic writings. One of the most renowned miracle workers with many miracles related to bringing rain was Choni Ha-Me'aggel. His life and examples of his miracles appear later in this volume.

The Descent of Fire upon the Altar at Mount Carmel (I Kings 18:38)

In chapter 18 of the First Book of Kings, Elijah meets and confronts King Ahab and his Phoenician wife Queen Jezebel.

In those days, it was high treason to proclaim the God of Israel. Both the king and queen permitted the worship of the god Baal. Against this dark setting, Elijah fearlessly pronounced the doom that would follow upon their apostasy and their outrage of justice.

Elijah the prophet challenged King Ahab and Queen Jezebel for their Baal worship, asking the Baal priests to come to Mount Carmel and there Elijah would demonstrate who the true God really is. Two altars were constructed on Mount Carmel. When the false priests offered sacrifices to Baal, the sacrifices were not consumed. Elijah then brought a sacrifice to God, which was miraculously burnt in answer to Elijah's prayer. The people then proclaimed God to be the One and only One in an overwhelming act of surrender. Their confession "Adonai hu ha-elohim" (God is the One and Only One) has become Israel's watchword, alongside the declaration of unity "Shema Yisrael" (Hear O Israel, the Lord is our God, the Lord is One). These words form the conclusion of the Day of Atonement service and are the last words traditionally uttered by a dying Israelite. Elijah, the timeless and deathless prophet, was the champion of purity of worship and justice to humanity.

The Splitting of the Waters of the Jordan (II Kings 2:8, 14)

In this story Elijah paid a farewell visit to Jericho and Beth El, centers of the sons of the prophets. He found himself alone with Elisha standing by the Jordan River, with fifty men of the sons of the prophets as eye witnesses. Elijah took his mantle, wrapped it together, and struck the water, which divided to the right and to the left, allowing them to cross over onto dry land. Later, after Elijah ascended to the heaven in a whirlwind, Elisha picked up Elijah's mantle and returned to the banks of the Jordan. Again, the waters parted to the right and to the left, and Elisha crossed over. When the disciples of the prophets at Jericho saw him from a distance, they exclaimed, "The spirit of Elijah has settled on Elisha!"

In this story Elisha was recognized as the successor of Elijah. His ability to perform the miracle of the parting of the waters using Elijah's mantle entitled him to this recognition.

The Cake Baked on Hot Stones and the Cruse of Water
(I Kings 19:1–8)

In this most amazing occurrence, Elijah fled from Queen Jezebel's vengeance. Running for his life, he arrived in Beersheba, a place where he believed he would remain safe from Jezebel's threat. Seeing the powerful influence which Jezebel still exercised despite Elijah's triumph on Mount Carmel, he lost hope of ever reforming King Ahab and the people. So he prayed for a release from the troubles and anxieties of an evil world. Lying down under a tree, he went to sleep. Here is the continuation of the story in the words of the Bible:

> An angel touched him, and said to him: "Arise and eat." And he looked, and behold, there was at his head a cake baked on the hot stones, and a cruse of water. He ate and drank, and laid himself down again. And the angel of God came again a second time, and touched him and said: "Arise and eat, because your journey is too great for you." And he arose and did eat and drink, and went on the strength of that meal forty days and forty nights to Horeb, the mountain of God.

In this miracle story, Elijah was provided by God's angel with food which, when eaten, sustained him for a remarkable period of forty days and nights. This is reminiscent of Moses, who, when atop Mount Sinai, likewise lived without food for the same number of days and nights (Exodus 34:28).

The Feeding of Elijah by Ravens (I Kings 17:6)

In this miracle story, Elijah warned King Ahab that according to the word of God there would be drought. God then told Elijah to turn eastward and hide by the brook of Cherith, a tributary of the Jordan River. It was there that God told Elijah to drink the water and that ravens would feed him. And so it was that ravens brought Elijah bread and meat, both in the morning and in the evening.

This is one of the few occasions in the entire Bible of an animal feeding a human being. Some modern commentators who were skeptical of this miracle and wanted to propose a rational explanation, have proposed the alteration of the Hebrew word for ravens *orvim* to *aravim*, meaning Arabs.

Vision of God at Mount Horeb (I Kings 19:10–12)

At a cave at Mount Horeb, the mountain on which God first appeared to Moses, the word of God came to Elijah:

> Elijah said: "I have been very jealous for the Lord, the God of Hosts, for the children of Israel have forsaken Your covenant, thrown down Your altars, slain Your prophets with the sword. I am the only one left, and they seek my life." And God said: "Go forth and stand upon the mountain of God." And behold, God passed by, and a great and strong wind rent the mountains, and broke the rocks in pieces. But God was not in the wind, and after the wind an earthquake, but God was not in the earthquake. And after the earthquake a fire, but

God was not in the fire. And after the fire a still small voice.
(Kings I:19:1–12)

This narrative is one of the most profound in all of the
Bible. In a beautifully acted parable, Elijah is taught the error
of his methods. The wind, fire, and earthquake in this story are
often spoken of as the heralds of God, and while they clearly
do act at times as God's agents, they do not disclose Him so
perfectly as the calm and serenity that follows the storm. Evil
is indeed mighty and loud, but it cannot be successfully
overcome by storm and fire. Rather, it is the gentle calmness
of God's voice that will ultimately bring healing and peace to
the world.

The implications for the modern worshiper at prayer services,
based upon this parable, are enormous. Our story suggests that
a worshiper ought to spend increased time listening carefully
to the still, small voice of the words of the prayer book, rather
than thinking only about chanting the words aloud. The more
one carefully listens, the more likely one will come to feel the
presence of God. One's life can be shaped by listening intently
to the sounds and the voices.

Elijah's Ascent to Heaven in a Whirlwind (II Kings 2:9–11)

The miraculous ascension of Elijah in a whirlwind to heaven
is graphically portrayed in the second chapter of Kings II:

> And it came to pass when they were gone over, that Elijah
> said to Elisha: "Ask what I shall do for you, before I am taken
> from you." And Elisha said: "I pray you, let a double portion of
> your spirit be upon me." And he said, "You have requested a
> difficult thing. Nevertheless, if you see me when I am taken
> from you, it shall be so to you. But if not, it shall not be so."

And it happened, as they still went on, and talked, that, there appeared a chariot of fire, and horses of fire, which parted them both asunder. And Elijah went up by a whirlwind to heaven.

Traditionally, the firstborn son was entitled to a double portion of his deceased father's estate, while the other sons each had a single portion. In this story Elisha, being Elijah's principal successor, asked for a double portion in the gift of prophecy which his master, so to speak, was bequeathing to the other prophets. It was indeed a difficult request, since the gift of prophecy is endowed by God and it is not the prerogative of one human being to bestow it upon another. Nevertheless, Elijah says that if Elisha is deemed worthy of witnessing the miracle of Elijah's departure, it would be an indication that he enjoyed God's favor and could take it as a token that his request would be granted by God. And so, Elijah miraculously departed to the heavens by a chariot and horses of fire in a whirlwind.

The deep impression left by Elijah's wondrous trip to heaven made Elijah a legendary figure both in biblical times and modern times as well. Because the Bible does not speak of his actual death, Elijah's presence and spirit continues to flourish in many Jewish life cycle events and rituals, including the circumcision (the "chair of Elijah"), at the Passover Seder ("Elijah's cup"), and at the close of the Havdalah ceremony at the conclusion of the Sabbath, when the Elijah the Prophet hymn is traditionally sung. Rabbinic literature, Jewish folklore, and mystical writings have portrayed Elijah as a prophet-angel whereby he can maintain identities both in heaven and on earth, performing wondrous deeds of kindness. The prophet Malachi, the last of the Jewish prophets, in his final prophecy predicted that Elijah would be sent by God "before the coming of the great and terrible day of the Lord," so that he may "turn the hearts of the fathers to the children, and the hearts of the children to their fathers" (Malachi 3:23). This prophecy became the point of departure for every subsequent association of Elijah as the one who would announce the coming of the Messiah.

Biblical Miracle Stories of Elisha

The Healing of the Waters of Jericho (II Kings 2:19–22)

After Elisha's recognition as the successor of Elijah, the men of Jericho who had learned of Elisha's supernatural powers related to him the problems with the bad water. This water caused frequent miscarriages by women and trees to shed their fruits before they were ripe.

> And Elisha said: "Bring me a new cruse, and put salt therein." And they brought it to him, and he went forth to the spring of the waters, and threw salt therein. Then he said: "Thus says God: I have healed these waters, there shall not be from thence any more death or miscarrying." So the waters were healed unto this day, according to the word of Elisha which he spoke.

The miraculous ability to heal the waters was one of Elisha's first miracles. The Ain es-Sultan, a fountain of sweet and tasty water rising at the foot of the ruins of the ancient city, is sometimes called the "Fountain of Elisha," and there can be little doubt that its name is derived from our story of the healing of the bad waters of Jericho.

The Killing of the Youths by the Bears (II Kings 2:23–24)

In the very next Elisha miracle story after the healing of the Jericho waters, Elisha traveled to Beth El where he was mocked by city children who referred to him as a bald head. When Elisha saw them, he cursed them in God's name. Because of the curse, two she-bears emerged from the woods and injured forty-two of the children.

There is extensive commentary on the reasons for Elisha's curse. One rabbinic thinker (Sotah 46b) has explained the use of the noun bald head as denoting that the children were "bare (*menuarim*) of divine commandments," meaning that they were irreligious. Other modern scholars have cited the fact that in the East baldness was considered a disgrace. Still other commentators asserted that the children were contrasting Elisha's baldness with Elijah's abundance of hair, thus derisively telling him to prove his claim to being Elijah's successor by ascending to heaven as Elijah his master had done.

The Filling of the Trenches with Water without Wind or Rain
(II Kings 3:20)

In the story regarding preparations for an attack on Moab, a lack of water induced the king of Israel to appeal to Elisha. God's hand came upon Elisha and told him to dig trenches in the valley for collecting the water which would miraculously flow into them. God further told Elisha that although there would be no rain or wind, the valley would be filled with water, enough for both people and animals.

After the country had been filled with this miraculous water, the Moabites gathered themselves to fight against Israel. Another amazing occurrence took place:

They rose up early in the morning and the sun shone upon the water, and the Moabites saw the water come way off as red as blood. And they said: "This is blood: the kings have surely fought together, and they have killed each person his fellow person." Now therefore, Moab, to the spoil. And when they came to the camp of Israel, the Israelites rose up and killed the Moabites, so that they fled.

It appeared that since there had been no rain in their land near Moab, the Moabites, thinking that the valley must be dry, naturally imagined it to be full of blood. For rationalists analyzing this text, the notion of an optical illusion—the sun shining on the water "painting" it the color of blood—is a common one. Thinking that the kings must have fought among themselves and killed each other, they entered the Israelite camp believing that it would be easy to capture it. Much to their surprise, they were ambushed by the Israelites and attacked.

God's Blessing of Increase from the Pot of Oil of Obadiah's Widow (II Kings 4:1–7)

The Prophet Elisha sought every opportunity to practice loving kindness and to bring relief and blessing wherever he went in the course of his ministry. In the beginning of the fourth chapter of II Kings, we are presented with the following miraculous tale. A certain woman (commentators have identified her as the widow of Obadiah, the god-fearing minister of King Ahab, who sheltered the prophets when Jezebel persecuted them) incurred a severe debt which could not be repaid. As a result, the children of the woman were to be "collected" instead of the debt. It is here that Elisha came to her miraculous rescue:

Elisha said to her: "What shall I do for you? Tell me, what do you have in your house?" And she answered, "Your hand-maid has not anything except for a pot of oil." Then Elisha said: "Go, borrow vessels from neighbors, even empty ones. Go inside, shut the door upon you and your sons, and pour out into all those vessels. And you shall set aside that which is full." So she went from him, shut the door upon her and her sons. They brought the vessels to her, and she poured out. And it happened that when the vessels were full that she said to her son: "Bring me yet a vessel." And he said to her, "There are no more." And the oil stayed. Then she came and told the man of God. And he said, "Go and sell the oil and pay the debt and you and your children can live on the rest."

The Birth of the Son of the Shunammite Woman and his Resuscitation (II Kings 4:8–34)

In this miracle tale, Elisha befriended a Shunammite woman who was known to joyfully extend hospitality to him on his frequent journeys through that district. When Elisha learned that she could bear no children, he called to tell her that she would give birth to a son. Elisha's prediction came true, and miraculously she conceived and gave birth to a son. Later in the child's life after it had grown, Elisha was told that the child could not be awakened. When Elisha went to the house, he saw the dead child lying on his bed. Here is the end of the story as the Bible tells it:

Elisha went in, shut the door, and prayed to God. And he went up and lay upon the child, and put his mouth upon his mouth, and his eyes upon his eyes, and his hands upon his hands. And he stretched himself out upon him, and the child became warm. Then he returned, and walked in the house to and fro, and went up, stretching himself upon him. The child sneezed seven times and opened his eyes.

Aware that he could do nothing without the help of God, Elisha prayed to God, as Elijah had done on numerous occasions. Several biblical commentators, in an attempt to take the supernatural element out of the story, suggest that Elisha was one of the first persons recorded in the Bible to have performed mouth-to-mouth resuscitation.

The Curing of the Bitter Pottage of the Sons of the Prophets (II Kings 4:38–41)

When Elisha came to Gilgal, there was a famine in the land. Elisha instructed his servant to cook pottage for the sons of the prophets. One went out into the field to gather herbs and found a wild vine and gathered wild gourds and shred them all together into a pot. As they were eating, the bitter taste must have aroused the thought that they were being poisoned, and they told Elisha that "there was death in the pot." Elisha then told them to bring meal which he subsequently cast into the pot and the mixture in the pot was again edible.

After this occurrence, a man from Baal-shalishah brought Elisha bread of the first fruits, twenty loaves of barley and fresh ears of corn. When told by Elisha to give it to the people to eat, his servant wondered how it might be possible for this small amount of food to feed one hundred men. However, miraculously the men did have enough to eat. Either the quantity of bread had mysteriously increased or a fifth of a loaf more than satisfied the hunger of each man.

The Healing of Naaman's Leprosy (II Kings 5:1–14)

In this extraordinary episode, Naaman, captain of the host of the king of Arm, was stricken with leprosy and advised to go to Elisha for a cure. Elisha sent a messenger to him asking that he go and wash in the Jordan River seven times. But Naaman was angry and went away. He then asked, "Are not Aman and Phrapar, the rivers of Damascus better than all of the waters in Israel?" Subsequently convinced to return to the Jordan River, he immersed seven times according to Elisha's advice and emerged cured of his leprosy. He converted to the God of Israel and renounced all other gods when he said: "Behold, now I know that there is no God in all of the earth but in Israel."

The Floating of an Axhead upon the Water
(II Kings 6:1–7)

In this story, the sons of the prophets wished to dwell near the Jordan River. When they came to the Jordan, they cut down wood, but accidentally the axhead fell into the water. The one who dropped it was very upset and concerned because it had been borrowed. When Elisha was told what had happened, he told the person to cut down a stick and throw it in, making the axhead float. He was able to reach out and retrieve it.

The medieval commentator Kimchi explains in his commentary that the stick had been previously cut and shaped to fit into the ax. Thus the miracle consisted of the fact that when the stick was thrown into the water, it penetrated the hole of the axhead and kept the implement afloat.

The Smiting of the Samarian Army with Blindness and the Restoration of Sight through the Intercession of Prayer
(II Kings 6:18–20)

In this miracle story, a Samarian army detachment was sent to capture Elisha and was itself entrapped. Here is the story in the words of the Bible:

When they came down to him, Elisha prayed to God, and said: "Smite this people with blindness." And God smote them with blindness, according to the word of Elisha. And Elisha said to them: "This is not the way, neither is this the city. Follow me and I will bring you to the man whom you seek." And he led them to Samaria. And it came to pass when they came to Samaria that Elisha said: "Open the eyes of these men, that they may see." And God opened their eyes, and they saw, and behold, they were in the midst of Samaria.

The Confusion Caused by God in the Aramean Camp
(II Kings 7:6)

In this biblical story, four lepers decided to enter the enemy's lines where they would have at least a chance of survival. But even if they should be killed, they would be no worse off, since in their present state death was almost a certainty. All available food had been consumed, and even the refuse of the streets was sold at famine prices. The king blamed the Prophet Elisha for all of these calamities, and the king was determined to put him to death. However, when faced by Elisha, he was overawed. Elisha made the astonishing announcement that the next day God would send relief and the famine would break. When the lepers went into the Aramean camp, they were totally taken by surprise. God had miraculously made the army of the Arameans hear the noise of chariots, horses, and an army. They thought it to be kings of the Hittities and Egyptians whom the Israelites had hired. The Arameans, panic-stricken that they were entrapped by the enemy, left everything intact (including the animals) and fled their camp totally confused. Thus the lepers had food, clothing, and shelter.

The Resurrection of the Man Who Came into Contact with Elisha's Bones (II Kings 13:21)

In Elisha's last hours, he fell very sick. His courage and amazing spirit passed in one final effort to stimulate resistance to Syria. He joined with King Joash in an act prophetic of victory—the launching of the archer's missiles. However, the king failed him through a lack of persistence and Elisha the patriot died with misgivings as to the future of the country. Then came the miracle of all miracles:

> Now the bands of Moabites used to invade the land at the coming of each year. Once a man was being buried when the people caught sight of such a band, so they threw the corpse into Elisha's grave and went away. When the dead man came into contact with Elisha's bones, he came to live and stood up. (II Kings 13:20–21)

Thus ended the life of Elisha with the crowning miracle of his career, the revival and resurrection of a dead man.

Other Miraculous Signs of God

Signs (in Hebrew *otot*) are extraordinary and surprising events which God brings about to demonstrate His power and will in a particular situation when a person or people are in need of convincing. Sometimes a sign was given as proof of prophecy. The altar at Beth El collapsed as a sign that the prophecy of its future destruction was true (I Kings 13:1–6). Here are several other noteworthy signs made by God to prove His power:

The Burning Bush (Exodus 3:1–4)

It was in the desert that Moses experienced the wondrous and commanding presence of God while tending his flock. An angel of God pointed Moses in the direction of the burning bush that was not consumed by its own fire. Here is the story from the Bible:

> An angel of God appeared to him in a blazing fire out of a bush. Moses gazed, and there was a bush all aflame, yet the bush was not consumed. Moses said: "I must turn aside to look at the marvelous sight. Why doesn't the bush burn up?" When God saw that he had turned aside to look, God called to him out of the bush: "Moses, Moses." He answered, "Here I am. . . ."

It has been noted that in this story of the burning bush, God may have been testing Moses' attention span. Was this revelation through fire designed merely to attract Moses' attention, to make him look and stare, to shock and prepare him for what was to come? Or was the bush really meant to be symbolic, subject to both a general and a detailed interpretation? Some have said that the bush symbolized puny Israel threatened with destruction by the fire of Egyptian persecution. Other commentators have suggested that the lowly bush was presented as God's fire to show Moses that there is no place without God's presence, not even a thornbush. Whatever the case, Moses clearly seemed to get the message. By saying "hineni" (reminiscent of Abraham who answered similarly when told by God's angel to put down his knife and to not sacrifice his son Isaac), Moses indicated that he was prepared to listen to God and to learn of the mission that he would be asked to execute.

The sign of the bush (*hasneh ayneu ukal*—"and the bush was not consumed") is currently used as the logo of the Jewish Theological Seminary of America, home of the Conservative branch of Judaism. Its publishing arm is called the "Burning Bush."

Aaron's Rod Becomes a Serpent (Exodus 7:10)

In this story, Moses was told that when Pharaoh spoke to him and asked for a wonder, that he should tell Aaron to take his rod, cast it onto the ground, and it would become a serpent. The reader is surprised to learn that after the rod of Moses turned into a serpent, Pharaoh called his sacred wizards who were also able to turn their rods into serpents. However, Aaron's rod swallowed up all the rods of the Egyptian magicians.

Since the account in this story specifically states that the Egyptians used their own "enchantments" and "secrets," it appears that the serpent mystery was a standard item among Egyptian magicians. The ancient commentators Ibn Ezra, Maimonides, and Abrabanel stated that the serpent trick was simply an illusion. Other recent rationalists who have attempted to explain the serpent mystery, have stated that the stick is a snake at the very start. The snake is the Egyptian cobra, and one of its peculiarities is that it can be made motionless by putting pressure just below the head. When temporarily paralyzed, it becomes rigid like a stick, but when thrown to the ground, it is jolted back into action.

If one looks more carefully at the text, one sees that God appeared to explain the so-called snake trick to Moses: "Thus God said to Moses: 'Put out your hand and grasp the snake *by the tail*.' Moses put out his hand and seized it and it became a staff in his hand" (Exodus 4:3). Here is a clear suggestion that the snake became a staff when Moses grasped it by the tail, perhaps even swinging it around his head. Thus we have God explaining the trick to Moses!

The Test of the Staffs (Numbers 17:16–24)

After Korach and his followers tried to wrest the leadership from Moses, they were killed by an earthquake. However, more persuasion was necessary if all the Israelites were to be thoroughly convinced that Aaron had been chosen above "God's people" (Number 17:6). The test of the staff was created to settle this issue of doubt once and for all. Here is how the Bible tells it:

> God spoke to Moses saying: "Speak to the Israelites and take from them, from the chieftains of their ancestral houses, one staff for each chieftain of an ancestral house: twelve staffs in all. Inscribe each person's name on his staff . . . also inscribe Aaron's name on the staff of Levi. Deposit them in the Tent of Meeting before the Pact, where I meet you. The staff of the person whom I choose shall sprout, and I will rid myself of the constant complaints of the Israelites against you. . . ." The next day Moses entered the Tent of the Pact, and there the staff of Aaron of the house of Levi had sprouted: it had brought forth sprouts, produced blossoms, and borne almonds. (Numbers 17:16–24)

Throughout history, rods have been used as symbols of authority (the scepter of a monarch, the baton of an orchestra conductor, and so forth). Aaron's staff, which had been turned into a snake and had been the signal for turning the Nile River into blood, was probably a fairly ordinary stick. In the story of the test of the rods, the Bible clearly interprets the overnight budding of Aaron's rod as nothing short of a miracle. Late legends (such as the stick of Joseph and Arimathea and that of Hercules) continue to use the theme of the sprouting stick.

The Midrash (Numbers Rabbah 18:23) says that the same staff of Aaron will be destined to be held in the hand of the King Messiah.

Bilaam's Talking Donkey (Numbers 22:22–30)

In this most incredible biblical story, the pagan prophet Bilaam was sent by Balak, King of the Moabites, to put a curse on the Israelites. Belief in the power of curses was very strong in biblical times, and even God viewed Bilaam's intent with grave alarm. As Bilaam was riding on his donkey, the donkey caught sight of God's angel standing in the way with drawn sword. The donkey swerved from the road and went into the field, and Bilaam beat it to return. After several beatings with a stick, God opened the mouth of the donkey:

> "What have I done to you that you have beaten me three times?" Bilaam said to the donkey: "You have made a mockery of me. If I had a sword with me, I'd kill you." The donkey then said to Bilaam, "Look, I am the donkey that you have been riding all along until this day. Have I been in the habit of doing thus to you?" And he answered, "No."

Traditional Jewish commentators have considered the speaking donkey which rebukes Bilaam a miraculous wonder, and its speech a wonder designed to magnify God's name and to demonstrate God's eternal love of the children of Israel. It is God who gives and controls speech, both in humans and animals. Maimonides, the medieval commentator, tried to rationalize the intent of the story, holding the opinion that Bilaam experienced the whole episode as a vision and that it really did not happen. Even more amazing than the donkey speaking is the miraculous fact that it perceived the angel of God, whereas Bilaam the prophet did not.

The lampooning of Bilaam in this story by the use of a talking donkey not only serves to downgrade his reputation but to demonstrate that one who was intent on putting a curse on the Israelites without the expressed consent of God was nothing more than a fool.

The Cloud of Glory (Exodus 13:21–22)

After the Sea of Reeds split and the Israelites safely passed through, the Bible informs us that God was with them by day in a pillar of cloud, to lead the way for them, and by night in a pillar of fire, to give them light.

Various attempts have been made to find a natural basis for the cloud. One theory is that the pillar was a brazier or a torch used to lead the caravan at night. But since these fires were not used during the day, it does not seem that the pillar of cloud can be explained as smoke. Some contend that the pillar was a volcano erupting to the east of the Israelites. During the day the smoke spewing from its cone could be seen, while at night the molten lava alone was visible. The main drawback to this theory is that there were no known active volcanoes existing along the route of the exodus.

Clearly, the cloud in its fiery appearance was a sign of God's presence to the Israelites. The cloud has come to be viewed as God's messenger and a manifestation of God's mercy and divine protection.

The Sun and Moon Stayed (Joshua 10:12)

In another celestial miracle in the Book of Joshua, the sun and moon were made to stop for one day. Here is the miracle according to the Bible:

> Then Joshua spoke to God in the day when God delivered the Amorites before the children of Israel. And he said in the sight of Israel: "Sun, stand still upon Gibeon. And you, moon, in the valley of Aijalon." And the sun stood still and the moon stayed.

One scientist, Immanuel Velikovsky, has attempted to explain the miracle of the staying of the sun and moon in his book *Worlds in Collision*. He argues that a comet passing extremely close to the earth could produce such effects, however, this book has not been particularly well-received by astronomers. Some have argued that the darkening of the sun was an eclipse.

There is no doubt that the Book of Joshua recognizes that a great miracle had occurred: "And there was no day like that before it or after it, that God had listened to the voice of a man, for God fought for Israel" (Joshua 10:14).

MIRACLES IN THE TALMUD

Miracles do not happen every day. (Talmud Pesachim 50b)

Although the Bible has no word corresponding to the English word *miracle*, the almost universal word for a miracle in rabbinic writings is the term *nes* which in the Bible is used for a *sign*. The miracles in the Bible are for the most part accepted as such by the Talmudic sages. However, at the same time, they do not emphasize belief in them as fundamental to the faith. Miracles, which occupy such a conspicuous place in the New Testament and in the history of Christianity, are viewed as matters of secondary importance throughout the rabbinic literature.

In all rabbinic literature there is not a single time that a rabbi was asked by his colleagues to demonstrate the soundness and validity of a particular doctrine or the truth of a disputed halachic case by performing a miracle. Only once do we hear of Rabbi Eliezer (Talmud Baba Metzia 59) who had recourse to miracles for the purpose of showing that his conception of a certain Jewish law was the right one. In this one instance, the majority declined to accept the miraculous intervention as a demonstration of truth and decided against the rabbi who appealed to it. Not a single miracle is accorded

61

to any of the great rabbis such as a Hillel or Shammai who influenced a large body of Jewish law and a cadre of students.

THE PREORDINATION OF MIRACLES

According to a number of rabbis, biblical miracles were preordained and were provided for in the act of creation rather than being an interruption of God's order of creation. The following is a cross section of Talmudic opinion as it relates to the preordination of miracles.

1. Rabbi Jochanan said: "The Holy God, blessed be the One, made a stipulation with the sea that it should divide before Israel. Thus it is written, And the sea returned 'to its strength' [Exodus 14:27], according to its agreement." Rabbi Jeremiah ben Eleazar said: "Not only with the sea did God make a stipulation, but with everything that was created in the six days of creation, as it is written, 'I, even my Hands have stretched out the heavens, and all their host have I commanded [Isaiah 45:12]. I commanded the sea to divide, and the heavens to be silent before Moses, as it says, Give ear you heavens, and I will speak [Deuteronomy 32:1]. I commanded the sun and the moon to stand still before Joshua; I commanded the ravens to feed Elijah; I commanded the fire to do no hurt to Hananiah, Mishael, and Azariah. I commanded the lions not to harm Daniel, the heavens to open up before Ezekiel and the fish to spew forth Jonah'" (Genesis Rabbah 4:5).

2. When God commanded Moses to raise his staff and divide the Red Sea, Moses argued with God that it would involve a breach of His own act of creation. Here

is the line of argumentation as portrayed in the Midrash of Exodus 21:6:

Moses said to the Holy One, blessed be He: "You commanded me to divide the sea and convert it to dry ground. But have you not written, Who has placed the sand for the bound of the sea [Jeremiah 5:22] and have You not sworn that You will never divide it?" Rabbi Eleazar Hakkapar said: "Moses asked God: 'Did You not promise that the sea would not be changed into dry land, for it says, "Who has placed the sand for the bound of the sea?" And does it not say, Or who shut up the sea with doors?' [Job 38:8]. God's reply was: "You have not read the Torah from the beginning, where it is written, 'And God said: Let the waters under the heaven be gathered together' [Genesis 1:9]. It was I who made a condition at the very beginning that I would one day divide it. For it says, 'And the sea returned to its strength when the morning appeared' [Exodus 14:27], that is, in accordance with the condition which I made with it at its creation. . . ." (Exodus Rabbah 21:5)

3. The Mishneh of the Ethics of the Fathers lists the ten miracles created on the eve of the first Sabbath of creation at twilight. Here are the words of the Ethics of the Fathers 5:6:

Ten miracles were wrought for our ancestors in the Temple: no woman miscarried from the scent of the holy meat; the holy meat never turned putrid; no fly was seen in the slaughter house; no unclean accident ever happened to the High Priest on the Day of Atonement; the rain never quenched the fire on the woodpile on the altar; no wind prevailed over the column of smoke that arose from it; never was a defect found in the *omer*, or in the two loaves, or in the showbread; the people stood pressed together, yet bowed themselves at ease, never did serpent or scorpion do harm in Jerusalem, and no person ever said to his fellow human being: 'The place is too crowded for me that I should lodge in Jerusalem.'

The ten miracles previously enumerated in connection with the Temple and Jerusalem are not mentioned at all in the Bible. They were woven about the Temple and Jerusalem, the Holy City, by folklore, because of the great respect and love the Jews had for them.

MIRACLES ARE NOT MEANT TO DEMONSTRATE A RELIGIOUS TRUTH

In this next example the rabbis attempted to demonstrate the biblical opinion that miracles are not proof or evidence of a religious truth. The Bible says it succinctly:

If there arises in the midst of you a prophet, or a dreamer of dreams, and he gives you a sign or a wonder. And the sign or the wonder comes to fruition, whereof he spoke to you—saying: "Let us go after other gods, which you have not known, and let us serve them." You shall not listen to the words of that prophet, or to the dreamer of dreams, for God puts you to proof, to know whether you do love the Lord your God with all of your heart and with all of your soul. (Deuteronomy 13:2–4)

In essence the Bible is saying that the fulfillment of the prediction of a prophet is not evidence of the validity of the prophet's claims. God is putting one to the test to see whether one's loyalty to God can withstand the most treacherous seductions from His revealed will. This refusal by the Bible to recognize a miracle as necessarily a proof of the truth of a doctrine is typically Jewish.

Here is a remarkable story from the Talmud which tells how Rabbi Elixir, once being unable to convince his colleagues of the correctness of his opinion, performed a number of miracles without the slightest success in swaying them to his side. In this story Rabbi Elixir ben Harkens calls for and achieves a series of miracles for the purpose of proving that a particular Jewish legal ruling is correct. However, as the story bears out, this hypothesis is rejected:

> On that day Rabbi Elixir brought forward every imaginable argument, but they did not accept them. He said to them: "If the *Holyoke* (i.e., the law) agrees with me, let this carob tree prove it." Thereupon the carob tree was torn a hundred cubits out of its place—others affirm, four hundred cubits. "No proof can be brought from a carob tree," they retorted. Again he said to them, "If the *Holyoke* agrees with me, let the stream of water prove it." Whereupon the stream of water flowed backwards.
>
> "No proof can be brought from a stream of water," they answered. Again he urged: "If the *Holyoke* agrees with me, let the walls of the schoolhouse prove it," whereupon the walls inclined to fall. But Rabbi Joshua rebuked them saying, "When scholars are engaged in a *halachic* dispute, what have you to interfere?" Hence they did not fall, in honor of Rabbi Joshua, nor did they resume the upright, in honor of Rabbi Elixir. And they are still standing thus inclined.
>
> Again he said to them: "If the *Holyoke* agrees with me, let it be proven from Heaven." Whereupon a heavenly voice cried out: "Why do you dispute with Rabbi Elixir, seeing that

in all matters the *Holyoke* agrees with him." But Rabbi Joshua arose and said: "It is not in heaven." What did he mean by this? Rabbi Jeremiah said: "That the Torah had already been given at Mount Sinai. We pay no attention to a Heavenly voice, because You have long since written in the Torah at Mount Sinai, After the majority once must incline." [Exodus 23:2] (Talmud Baba Metzia 59b)

EVERYDAY MIRACLES OF LIFE

The rabbis also emphasized the daily miracle of life. There is no necessity in expressing the fact that God violates His own laws of nature. On several occasions the daily wonders of divine providence were extolled by rabbinic thinkers above the biblical miracles. Here are several citations expressing daily miracles which do not involve a disturbance of the order of creation.

1. Come and see how many miracles God performs for humans but they do not realize it. If a person swallowed dry bread, it would go down into his bowels and scratch him. But God created a well in the throat which conducts the bread safely down (Exodus Rabbah 24:1).
2. In the thanksgiving prayer of the Amidah, the thought of daily miracles is expressed in the paragraph which states, "We thank You and praise You morning, noon, and night for Your miracles which daily attend us and for Your wondrous kindnesses."
3. Greater is the miracle that occurs when a sick person escapes from perilous disease than that which happened when Hananiah, Mishael, and Azariah escaped from the fiery furnace (Talmud *Nedarim* 41a).

4. The wonder of the support of a family in the midst of great distress is as great as the wonder of the parting of the Red Sea for Israel (Talmud *Pesachim* 118a).

ALLEGORICAL INTERPRETATION OF MIRACLES

One rabbinic method of explaining the biblical miracles was to allegorize them. The Midrash records numerous allegorical interpretations of biblical miracles that attest to the sages' rational trend of mind. For example, Rabbi Nehemiah wanted to explain the miracle at the Red Sea as a reward for Israel's trust in God. He deduced this from the passage: "And the people believed. . . ." [Exodus 4:31]. His colleague, Rabbi Isaac, however, being dissatisfied with such a rationalization, objected: "They saw all the miracles which were performed for them. How, then, could they not believe?" But matters were not left at that, for another sage, Rabbi Simeon the son of Abba, supported Rabbi Nehemiah's allegorizing attempt with the statement: "Still, it was because of Abraham's trust in the Holy One, Blessed be He, that they were privileged to sing the song at the Red Sea" (Exodus Rabbah 23:5).

Even more dramatic is the allegorical exposition of the biblical passage: "And it came to pass, when Moses held up his hand that Israel prevailed, and when he let down his hand, Amalek prevailed" (Exodus 17:11). The rabbis skeptically remarked: "Could then, the hands of Moses make the battle or break the battle?" And they decided that this action of Moses had only a symbol significance. "For as long as the Israelites looked upward and kept their hearts in submission to their Father in heaven, they prevailed; otherwise, they were defeated" (Talmud *Rosh HaShanah* 29a).

ONE MUST NOT RELY ON MIRACLES

Rabbinic opinion was such that people were constantly reminded not to depend on miracles. For instance, the Talmud *Pesachim* 64b states that "One is forbidden to rely upon miracles." The Talmud (*Taanit* 20b) states that "a person should never stand in a place of danger and say 'a miracle will happen to me' since perhaps it will not happen, and if it does, it will be deducted from his merits."

Shimon ben Shetach threatened Onias the saint with excommunication for his demonstrative appeal to God to send down the rain in a miraculous manner (Talmud *Taanit* 3:8). In a like manner Rabbi Shimon ben Shetach adjudged Choni, the mystical circle maker, as deserving excommunication when he produced much needed rain by means of magical prayers (Talmud *Taanit* 23a).

In another miracle story (Talmud *Shabbat* 53b), a woman died and left her poverty-stricken husband with an infant to care for. A miracle happened and his breasts opened up like the breasts of a woman so that he could nurse the child. Although Rabbi Joseph commented how great this man was that such a miracle was performed for him, the great rabbi Abaye objected saying, "On the contrary, how bad this man was that the world's order was changed on his account" (Talmud *Shabbat* 53b).

When asked by the Romans, "If your God is as omnipotent as you claim, why does He not destroy the idols?" the Jewish sages replied, "Shall God destroy sun, moon, and stars on account of the fools that worship them? The world goes on in its order and the idolators shall meet with their doom (Talmud *Avodah Zarah* 4:7).

THE AGE OF MIRACLES HAS CEASED

It was generally accepted during talmudic times that the age of miracles for the benefit of people had ended because they were not ready to make supreme sacrifices to God. This can be illustrated by these talmudic citations:

1. Rabbi Papa said to Abaye: How is it that for the former generations miracles were performed and for us miracles are not performed? It cannot be because of their superiority in study, because in the years of Rav Judah the whole of their studies was confined to Nizikin, and we study all six orders. . . . And yet when Rav Judah drew off one shoe, rain used to come, whereas we torment ourselves and cry loudly, and no notice is taken of us. He replied: The former generations used to be ready to sacrifice their lives for the sanctity of God's name. We do not sacrifice our lives for the sanctity of God's name (Talmud *Berachot* 20a).

2. What is meant by, When aforetime the land of Zebulun and the land of Naphtali did lighten its burden, but in later times it was made heavy by way of the sea, beyond Jordan, in Galilee of the nations? It is not as the early generations who rejected the yoke of the Torah; but as for the latter generations who strengthened the yoke of the Torah upon themselves and are therefore worthy of having a miracle wrought for them, like those who passed over the Red Sea and the Jordan (Talmud *Sanhedrin* 94b).

3. When Pappus and Lulianus were asked by their Roman executioners, "Why does your God not save you as He

did the three youths in Nebuchadnezzar's time?" they
replied, "We are probably not worthy of such a miracle"
(Talmud *Taanit* 18b).

PRESCRIBED BENEDICTIONS
WHEN APPROACHING PLACES
OF MIRACULOUS EVENTS

Ancient rabbinic thinkers prescribed benedictions to be
recited when approaching places made memorable by miraculous events. According to the talmudic tractate of *Berakhot*
9:1, when coming to a place where miracles were brought for
the Jewish people one must recite the following blessing:
"Blessed be He, who wrought miracles for our ancestors in this
place." The Talmud goes on to describe two instances when
Mar, the son of Rabina, had occasion to recite the blessing for
experiencing the miraculous. One was when he was going
through the valley of Aravot and was very thirsty. A well of
water was miraculously created for him and he drank. The
second instance was when he was going through the manor of
Machoza and a wild camel attacked him. At the moment the
camel attacked him, the wall of a nearby house fell in and he
escaped inside.

MIRACLE STORIES
IN RABBINIC WRITINGS

There are a variety of stories and tales in the writings of the
sages that relate to miraculous occurrences. The following is a
selection of them taken both from talmudic as well as
midrashic texts.

Wings of the Dove

Once the government decreed that the head of the one who wore *tefillin* should be broken. Elisha wore them on the street, and when an official ran toward him, he removed his *tefillin* and placed them in his hands.

"What is it that you have in your hands?" the official asked.

"A pair of pigeon's wings," Elisha replied. He opened his hands, and a pair of wings lay there.

Elisha bore in mind the words of the psalmist [Psalm 68:14]: "The wings of the dove are covered with silver." As the dove is protected by her own silver wings, so are the children of Israel protected by their *mitzvot* (Talmud *Shabbat* 19).

The Importance of Saying the Blessing over the Meal

If a person eats and forgets to say grace, that person is required to return to the place of the meal and recite it. Once a student forgot, and on returning, discovered a valuable article which nobody claimed. Another student left quickly without saying grace, intending to say it elsewhere. That person walked into a dangerous place and was injured.

Rabbah bar Chanah was traveling in a caravan. One day after completing his meal he forget to say the blessing. As he reminded himself he thought: "If I tell the leader the truth, he will say: 'Recite grace where you are, for, wherever you say grace, it is grace in the eyes of God.' I shall tell them that I have left behind a golden dove."

He did so and on his path, he found a dove. He exclaimed: "As the dove is protected by its wings, so are the children of Israel protected by their *mitzvot*."

The Miracle of the Golden Coins

A student of Rabbi Shimon ben Yochai departed for a foreign country where he grew rich. Upon returning, the other disciples were jealous and also wished to leave Palestine.

Their master said: "Come with me; I shall work for you a miracle, and the valley here shall be filled with gold coins. But you know of a truth, that you will have your reward either in the world or in the everlasting life. Make your choice" (Midrash Exodus Rabbah 52).

The Incredible Pearl

Rabbi Shimon ben Chalafta was very poor. On Passover he experienced a great commotion. "People are preparing for the festival," he was told. "Some already have money in their possession, and others secure it from their employers."

"I too will ask for something from my employer on account," thought Rabbi Shimon.

Lo and behold, a magnificent pearl appeared before his very eyes. He went to Rabbi Judah the Prince and the Rabbi said to him: "Accept a loan of three *dinarii* and later we shall auction the pearl."

Rabbi Shimon took the money to his wife and told her what had happened. She then remarked: "I do not wish your share in the world-to-come to be diminished. Give back the loan and return the pearl to your employer."

Rabbi Judah sent for her and said: "We, his comrades, will try to repay for your husband whatever he received on account. It is better for you to keep the sum and be relieved from poverty."

The pious woman still refused, however, on the plea that every *tzaddik* (righteous person) can work only for his reward.

He cannot share it with another. Her husband, Rabbi Shimon, thereupon laid down the pearl and it immediately disappeared into thin air (Midrash Ruth Rabbah 3).

The Golden Table Leg

The wife of Rabbi Chanina ben Dosa could not endure her poverty and sought her husband to pray for something on account. A golden table leg appeared in the room. Later, the rabbi's wife dreamed she was in Paradise. Each *tzaddik* had a home equipped with furniture of gold. Her husband's table, however, was missing a leg. When the rabbi's wife awakened she begged that the table leg be returned (Talmud *Taanit* 2).

The Incredible Shrinking Tithe

A farmer owned a field which produced 1000 measures of grain. He contributed 100 measures as a tithe, and from the balance he made a comfortable living.

When his son inherited the field, he also contributed 100 measures as tithe for the first year. The second year, however, he gave only 90 measures. The next season, his field produced only 900 measures of grain. Once again, he donated less tithe than he was required to give, and again the field produced less in exact proportion.

After a few years his kinsfolk heard that the field produced no more than 100 measures. They dressed in white garments and visited him.

The farmer said: "Have you come in holiday dress to rejoice over my bad fortune?"

"No, we came to offer you congratulations. Formerly you were the farmer and God was the *Kohen* (priest). Now, God is become the farmer and you have become the *Kohen*."

The Son of Pure Gold

Once Rabbi Abba declared in a discourse that every person that studies the Torah becomes rich. A young man named Yose took his words to mean material riches. He came to Rabbi Abba saying: "I wish to study in order to obtain these riches."

After a lapse of time, Rabbi Yose wanted to know when his wealth would accrue to him. Rabbi Abba was distressed to learn that this fine student was motivated by ulterior motives. He then said to him: "Continue to study, and if you must have material riches, I shall do my best to give them to you."

A wealthy youth entered the school and asked for Rabbi Abba, saying, "I have inherited great wealth. I appreciate the value of the study of Torah but my mind is not adapted to it. I wish to donate a vessel of pure gold to a fine student on condition that I shall have a share in his Torah." Rabbi Abba summoned Rabbi Yose and said to him, "Here is the first installment of your riches."

Soon thereafter, Rabbi Yose began to perceive the spiritual richness of the Torah, and he wept.

"Why do you weep?" asked his Master. Rabbi Jose replied, "Because I have sold true for apparent riches."

Rabbi Abba rejoiced in his heart. He recalled the rich youth and said: "The student regrets having accepted your gold. Take it back and give the money to the needy and orphaned, and it shall be accounted to you as if you had studied Torah as much as we."

Rabbi Yose was thrilled to dispense with the pure gold ("paz" in Hebrew), and he received the name of "Ben Pazzi," the "son of pure gold" (Zohar, part 1, pg. 88).

Ten Things Were Created by God on the Eve of the Sabbath of Creation at Twilight

1. the mouth of the earth (Korach and his followers were swallowed by the earth) [Numbers 16]
2. the mouth of the well (the Israelites drank water from this well in the desert) [Numbers 21:16]
3. the speech of the donkey (Bilaam's donkey had the power of speech) [Numbers 22]
4. the rainbow (after the flood Noah was shown a rainbow as a sign of God's covenant) [Genesis 9:13]
5. the manna
6. the rod (Moses used a rod in Egypt to bring about certain signs) [Exodus 4:17]
7. the shamir (a legendary worm which could eat the hardest stone)
8. the script (the writing on the tablets of the Ten Commandments)
9. the writing instrument (the implement with which the tablets were lettered)
10. the tablets (Ethics of the Fathers 5:8)

Ten Miracles Were Performed for Our Ancestors in the Temple

1. No woman miscarried from the scent of sacrificial meat.
2. The sacrificial meat never became putrid.
3. No fly was seen in the slaughter house.
4. The High Priest never became ritually impure on Yom Kippur.
5. The rains never extinguished the fire of the woodpile.
6. No wind dispersed the column of smoke.

7. No defect was found in the *omer*, the two loaves or the showbread.
8. The people stood pressed together, yet knelt in ease.
9. No scorpion or serpent ever injured anyone in Jerusalem.
10. No one complained, "It is too congested for me to lodge overnight in Jerusalem" (Ethics of the Fathers 5:7).

A *Rabbi Chanina ben Dosa* Miracle Story

Rabbi Chanina ben Dosa was carrying some salt when rain began to fall. He said in prayer: "Everyone feels pleasant, but Chanina does not." The rain stopped. Entering his home he said: "Everyone feels unpleasant except Rabbi Chanina." The rain came down once more.

Rabbi Chanina entered his home and discovered his daughter in tears. In error she had poured vinegar into the lamp on the eve of the Sabbath. He declared: "May the One who commanded the oil to burn also command the vinegar to burn." The vinegar burned all day after Havdalah. People came to Rabbi Chanina and said: "Your goats are doing damage."

Rabbi Chanina had some goats and was told that they were damaging people's property. He said: "If they really do damage, may bears devour them, but if not, may they bring the bears impaled on their horns." In the evening each of the goats brought a bear on its horns. (Talmud *Taanit* 24b)

Choni, the Rip Van Winkle of the Talmud

Rabbi Yochanan said: All his life long this righteous Choni was troubled about this verse: "When God brought back those that returned to Zion, we were like unto them that dream" (Psalms 126:1). Did anyone ever sleep seventy years nonstop?

One day while walking on the road he noticed a man planting a carob tree. Choni said to the man: "You know that it takes seventy years before a carob tree yields fruit. Are you certain that you will live seventy years and eat from it?"

"I found this world provided with carob trees," the man replied. "As my ancestors planted for me, so I plant for my children."

Thereupon Choni sat down to eat and was overcome by sleep. As he slept, a grotto was formed around him, so that he was screened over from humanity, and thus he slept for seventy years. When he awoke he saw a man gathering carobs from the carob tree and eating them. "Do you know who planted this carob tree?" Choni asked. "My grandfather," the man replied. "I must have slept seventy years!" Choni exclaimed. He then went to his home and asked whether the son of Choni the circle maker was still alive. "I am Choni," he said, but the people did not believe him. He took himself to the Bet HaMidrash where he heard the scholars say, "Our studies are as clear to us today as they used to be in the times of Choni the circle maker, for when he came to the Bet HaMidrash he used to explain to the scholars all of their difficulties."

He said to them: "I am Choni," but they would not believe him nor would they show him the respect due to him. He therefore prayed to God that he should die and he did indeed die (Talmud *Taanit* 23a).

Choni, the Circle Maker and Miraculous Rain Maker

Our rabbis have taught: It once happened that the great part of the month of Adar had passed by and no rain had fallen.

Choni, the circle maker, was therefore asked to pray for rain to fall. He did so, but no rain fell. He then drew a circle and placed himself in its center, as did the prophet Habbakuk, who said: "I will stand upon my watch" (Habbakuk 2:1). Choni said before God: "Master of the world. Your children have set their face upon me, because I am, as it were, Your intimate. I swear by Your great name that I will not move from here until You show mercy to Your children." Rain began to trickle. The people therefore said to him: "Master, we see you, and this is a warranty to us that we shall not die, but it seems to us that the rain comes only in order to free you from your oath." "You have seen me and you shall not die," Choni replied, and continuing his prayer said, "Not for such rain did I pray, but for rain sufficient to fill the cisterns and caves." The rain came down with great gusto, each drop as big as the opening of a barrel. The rabbis estimated that none of them contained less than a log. The people again said to him: "Master, we see you, and this is a warranty that we shall not die, but it seems to us that this rain comes only to destroy the world." "You have seen me and you shall not die," he replied, and then continued: "Not for such rain did I pray, but for a rain of benevolence, blessing, and mercy." The rain then continued coming in proper measure so that the Israelites had to go up from the streets of Jerusalem to the Temple mount on account of the rain.

They then said to him: "Just as you have prayed for the rain to come; so pray now for it to stop." He, however, replied, "I have a tradition that it is not proper to pray for the cessation of too much good. However, bring to me a bullock for the confession of my sins." They brought him a bullock, upon which Choni laid both his hands and said: "Master of the world. Your people Israel, whom You have brought out of Egypt, can stand neither too much good, nor too much punishment. When You became angry withholding rain, they could not stand it. Let it be Your desire that there be ease in the world."

Immediately the wind blew, the clouds dispersed and the sun began to shine and the people went out into the field and brought home morils and truffles (Talmud *Taanit* 23a).

The Miraculous Feeding of Rabbi Shimon bar Yochai and His Son

Rabbi Shimon bar Yochai and his son went and hid themselves in the Bet HaMidrash. His wife brought him bread and a jug of water and they dined. When the Roman decree of religious persecution increased in severity he said to his son, "Women are of unstable temperament. She may be put to the torture and expose us." So they proceeded to hide in a cave. A miracle occurred and a carob tree and a water well were created for them. They would strip their garments and sit up to their necks in sand. The whole day they studied. When it was time for prayers they dressed, covered themselves, prayed, and then took off their clothing again, so that they should not wear out. There they dwelt twelve years in the cave (Talmud *Shabbat* 33b).

Miraculous Breasts

Our rabbis taught: It once occurred that a man's wife died and left a child to be suckled, and he could not afford to pay a wet nurse. Whereupon a miracle occurred and his nipples opened like the two nipples of a woman and he suckled his son. Rabbi Joseph observed, "Come and see how great was this man, that such a miracle was performed on his account." Abaye said to him, "On the contrary, how lowly was this man,

that the order of creation was changed on his account"
(Talmud *Shabbat* 53b).

The Miraculous Rescue of the Three Men

Rabbi Shimon the Shilonite lectured: When the evil Nebuchadnezzar cast Hananiah, Mishael, and Azariah into the
fiery furnace, Yurkami, the Prince of hail, rose before the Holy
One, blessed be He, and said to Him: "Sovereign of the
Universe. Let me go down and cool the furnace and save these
righteous men from the fiery furnace." Gabriel said to him,
"The might of the Holy One, blessed be He, is not thus
manifested, for you are the Prince of hail, and all know that
water extinguishes fire. But I, the Prince of fire, will go down
and cool it within and heat it without, and will thus perform
a double miracle." The Holy One blessed be He said to him:
"Go down." It was then that Gabriel began with praise and
said, "And God's truth endures forever" (Talmud *Pesachim*
118a,b).

The Miracle of King Solomon's Trees

When King Solomon built the sanctuary, he planted therein
all kinds of trees of golden delights, which were bringing forth
their fruits in their season. As the winds blew at them, they
would fall off, as it is written, "May his fruits rustle like
Lebanon" (Psalm 57:16). When the foreigners entered the
Temple they withered, as it is written: "And the flower of
Lebanon languishes" (Nachum 1:4). The Holy One, Blessed
be He, will in the future restore them, as it is said: "It shall
blossom abundantly and rejoice, even with joy and singing,
the glory of Lebanon shall be given to it" (Isaiah 35:2).
Permanent miracles He does not include in His count. Now

that we have reached this conclusion, the ark and the cherubim are also permanent miracles (Talmud *Yoma* 21b).

Nicanor's Miraculous Doors

Our rabbis taught: What miracles happened to his doors? It was reported that when Nicanor had gone to fetch doors from Alexandria of Egypt, on his return a gale arose in the sea to drown him. Thereupon they took one of his doors and hurled it into the sea and yet the sea would not stop raging. When they prepared to throw the other one into the sea, he rose and clung to it saying, "Throw me in with it." They did so and the sea immediately stopped its raging.

He was deeply upset about the other door. Arriving at the harbor of Acco, the door broke through and came up from under the sides of the boat. Others say, a sea monster swallowed it and spat it out on the dry land. Touching this door, Solomon said: "The beams of our houses are cedars, and the panels are cypresses" (Song of Songs 1:17). Do not read "berothim" (cypresses) but "brit yam" (covenant of the sea). Therefore, all of the Sanctuary gates were changed for gold ones with the exception of the Nicanor gates because of the miracles wrought with them (Talmud *Yoma* 38a).

The Ark That Took Up No Space

Rabbi Levi further said: We have a tradition from our ancestors that the ark took up no room. It has been taught to the same effect: The ark which Moses made had round about it an empty space of ten cubits on every side. Now it is written, And in front of the sanctuary was twenty cubits in length and twenty in breadth (I Kings 6:20). It is also written, And the wing of the one cherub was ten cubits and the wing of the other cherub was ten cubits (I Kings 6:24). Where then was the ark itself? We must therefore conclude that it stood by a miracle (without taking up any room) (Talmud *Megilla* 10b).

The Wondrous Thorn

Rabbi Joseph expounded: How is the verse "I give thanks to You, O God. Although you were angry with me, Your anger has turned back, and You comfort me" (Isaiah 12:1) to be understood? Here the Bible alludes to two competitors who were about to go on a trading venture when a thorn got caught in the foot of one of them. He began to curse and blaspheme. After some time, however, when he learned that his competitor's ship had sunk in the sea, he began to thank God and glorify God (for having spared his life). Thus, "Your anger has turned back, and You comfort me." In this connection, Rabbi Eleazar said: What is implied in the verse "Who does wondrous things alone . . . Blessed be His glorious name forever?" (Psalm 72:18–19). That even he for whom the miracle is wrought is not aware of the miracle wrought for him (Talmud *Niddah* 31a).

The Miraculous Healing by God, An Everyday Miracle

Rabbi Alexandri said in the name of Rabbi Chiyya bar Abba: "The miracle wrought for a sick person is greater than the miracle wrought for Hananiah, Mishael, and Azariah. The miracle for these three men involved an ordinary fire lit by a human being, but the fire of fever of a sick person is from Heaven—who is able to extinguish that?" (Talmud *Nedarim* 41a).

The Miraculous Slaying of the Hosts of Sennacherib

Pharoah, the King of Egypt and Tirhakah, King of Ethiopia, who had come to help Hezekiah, benefited from a miracle. Before they reached Hezekiah, Sennacherib became aware that they were coming. What did he do to them? He captured them and put them in fetters. At midnight the angel went forth and killed the army of Sennacherib. When Hezekiah arose in the morning and found the two kings in fetters, he said, "It seems that the two had come to help me." So of course he released them, and both of them went forth to tell the miracles and wondrous acts of the Holy One (Midrash, Song of Songs Rabbah 4:8).

The Mountain on Top of the Mountain

"The mount of the mount" (Numbers 20:22)—means a mount on top of another mount, like a small apple on top of a large apple. Even though the cloud that went before Israel leveled heights and raised valleys, nevertheless the Holy One left this mount on top of a mount as a token to remind Israel of the miracles the Holy One had performed for them. For in order that Israel not become tired from going up and down mountains, the Holy One left no mountain standing in the desert. There were, however, important exceptions. Even though the cloud turned the wilderness into a plain, it always left one elevated area for the tabernacle to encamp upon. And it also left these mountains standing: Mount Sinai for the Presence, Mount Nebo as the burial place of Moses, and the mount on the mount as a burial place for Aaron (Tanchuma 37).

Miracles in the Valley of Arnon

"Spring up, o well, sing to it" (Numbers 21:17). What were
the miracles in the valley of Arnon that inspired Israel to sing
"spring up, o well"? A person could stand on top of a mountain
on one side of the valley and speak to a friend seven miles
away on top of a mountain on the other side. The road to the
Promised Land ran down to the valley between these two
mountains, and then ascended, for Israel's path lay through
several valleys. At that place, endless armies of all the nations
gathered, some of them taking up positions within the valley.
The mountain on one side of the valley was filled with caves.
Facing these caves in the mountain on the other side of the
valley there were numerous rocks, projecting breastlike formations.

The armies entered the caves figuring: "When Israel goes
down into the valley, our men that are stationed there will
confront them, while here, our men high up in the staves will
strike them from the rear, and so we shall kill them all."

However, when Israel reached that spot, the Holy One did
not make it necessary for them to go down into the valley, for
God beckoned to the mountains [and they came together],
the "breasts" of one mountain entering into the opposite caves
of the other, so that all within the caves were killed.
Moreover, the two mountains brought their summits close to
each other, forming a road so level that it was impossible to
tell one mountain from the other.

This valley formed the boundary between Israel and Moab.
The mountain in the land of Moab, containing the caves, did
not move, while the mountain from Israel, with its pointed
rocks resembling breasts, moved and locked with the mountain facing it. Why was it the one to move? Because it
belonged to the Land of Israel.

After the rocks had entered the caves and crushed all the mighty fighters within them, the well came down into the valley and its water swelled. It drowned the armies stationed there, even as the Red Sea had drowned the Egyptians. Israel passed over the top of the mountains without being aware of these miracles. The Holy One said: "I will not let the children of Israel know how many armies I destroyed for their sake." So the well, flowing down into the caves, flushed out skulls, arms, and legs. Subsequently, when Israel returned to look for the well, they saw it in the midst of the valley shining like the moon, still bringing up the limbs of the fighters. Then Israel, standing over the valleys, sang a song about the well: "Spring up, O well, sing to it" (*Tanchuma Hukkat* 47).

The Miracle of the Bathhouses

When Rabbi Samuel bar Nachman went down to bathe, he saw Rabbi Yudan the Patriarch standing in front of the great house of study, his face very pale. Rabbi Samuel asked: "Why is your face so pale?" Rabbi Yudan replied, "Such-and-such an order has been sent to me by the Roman government." Rabbi Samuel: "Come down and bathe, for your Creator will perform miracles for you." When the two entered the bathhouse, a bath sprite came jesting and dancing toward them. Rabbi Yudan the Patriarch wished to scold him, but Rabbi Samuel bar Nachman said, "Master, leave him alone, for sometimes he shows himself before miracles." Then to the sprite: "Your master is in trouble, yet you stand here joking and dancing." The sprite: "Eat and drink and keep the Sabbath with good cheer, for your God will perform miracles for you and I will set you before the emperor immediately after the conclusion of the Sabbath."

At the end of the Sabbath, immediately after the service, the sprite took them and set them in front of the gate. When the emperor was told, "Lo, they are standing before the gate," he ordered: "Close the gate." At that, the sprite took them and set them in the middle of the town. When the emperor was informed he exclaimed, "I command that the bathhouse be heated for seven days and seven nights. Then have them enter and bathe, and after that appear before me."

Accordingly, the bathhouse was heated for seven days and seven nights, but the sprite entered and tempered the heat for them, so that when they entered it they could bathe. Afterward they appeared before the emperor, who said to them, "Because you know that God performs miracles for you, you insult the emperor." They answered: "We did insult Diocletian the swineherd, but to Diocletian the emperor we willingly submit." "Even so," the emperor answered, "you should not insult the humblest Roman citizen or the lowest ranking Roman soldier" (Jerusalem Talmud, *Terumot* 8:8 and Genesis Rabbah 63:8).

The Miraculous Rescue of the Boys in the Nile River

"Every male that is born you shall throw into the Nile" (Exodus 1:22). Rabbi Chanan said: "What did the chaste and virtuous women do? They took their infants and hid them in holes in their houses. So the wicked Egyptians would take their own young children, bring them into the Israelite homes, and pinch their young until they cried. When the Israelite infants in their hiding places heard the Egyptian children cry, they cried with them. Then the Egyptians would seize the Israelite babies and cast them into the Nile."

At that time the Holy One said to the ministering angels: "Descend from my Presence and look at the children of My beloved Abraham, Isaac, and Jacob being thrown into the river." The ministering angels rushed headlong down from His Presence, and, standing up to their knees in the water, caught the children of Israel in their arms and set them upon rocks. Then out of each rock the Holy One brought forth nipples, which suckled the Israelite children (Midrash, Song of Songs Rabbah 2:15).

The Miracle on Account of the Righteous Women

Rabbi Akiba expounded: Israel was redeemed from Egypt on account of the righteous women of that generation. When they went to draw water, the Holy One for their sake caused so many small fish to be scooped up into their pitchers that only half of what they drew up was water and the other half fish. They would then heat two pots, one with hot water, and the other with fish, both of which they brought to their husbands in the field. There the women washed their husbands, annointed them, fed them, and gave them to drink. Then, lying secluded between mounds in the field, they responded to their men. After that, they returned to their homes. When the time for giving birth came, they went into the fields and gave birth under an apple tree, as it is written "Under an apple tree I roused you; there your mother was in labor with you, there was she in labor and brought you forth" (Song of Songs 8:50).

Then from the heights of heaven the Holy One sent an angel, who cleansed the infants and massaged their bodies as a midwife does in order to make a child look beautiful. Then God selected for each of them two breast-shaped stones, one filled with honey and the other with oil, as it is written, "And God made him such honey out of the crags, and oil out of the flinty rock" (Deuteronomy 32:13). When the Egyptians became aware of these babies, they came to kill them. But then a second miracle occurred, for the infants were swallowed up by the ground. At that, the Egyptians brought oxen and plowed the area where they had disappeared. But as soon as the Egyptians left, the babies burst forth out of the ground like grass in the field! As the infants grew up, they came running to their homes in flocks.

Later, when God revealed Himself at the Red Sea, these infants (now grown up) were the first to recognize God, for they said, "This is my God" (Exodus 15:2); (Talmud *Sotah* 11b; Exodus Rabbah 1:12).

The Miraculous Light of the Israelites in Egypt

The Bible says: "But all the children of Israel had light in their dwellings" (Exodus 10:23). The Bible does not say, "In the land of Goshen," but "in their dwellings," to show that wherever a Jew entered, light entered with him and illuminated for him what was in casks, chests, and hidden depositories (Midrash Exodus Rabbah 14:3).

The Miraculous Voice of God

"Go, return to Egypt" (Exodus 4:9). Rabbi Reuben said: "When the Holy One told Moses in Midian, 'Go, return to Egypt,' the command was divided into two distinct voices and assumed two distinct personae. Moses heard one voice saying in Midian, 'Go, return to Egypt'; while Aaron in Egypt heard the other voice saying, 'Go into the desert to meet Moses'" (Exodus 4:27). Thus, "God thunders miraculously in two places with His voice" (Job 37:5; Midrash Exodus Rabbah 5:9).

The Miracle of the Oil in the Temple

When the Greeks entered the Temple Hall, they defiled all the oils that were in it. Thus, when the royal house of the Hasmoneans grew strong and defeated the Greeks, they searched in the Temple and found only one jug of oil that had the seal of the high priest intact on it. There was enough oil in it for only one day's lighting. But a miracle occurred, and with that oil a lamp was lit for eight days. The following year, these eight days were fixed in the calendar as festive days to be celebrated with Hallel and thanksgiving (Talmud *Shabbat* 21b).

The Assassination of Caligula

On the twenty-second of Shevat the decree requiring the worship of idols which the enemy intended to bring into the Temple Hall was nullified. On that day, there is no public mourning.

The news that on a certain day Caligula had sent idols to be set up in the Temple Hall reached Jerusalem on the eve of the first day of Tabernacles. Shimon the Mild said: Observe the days of your Festival with happiness, for not one of the things you heard will come to pass. For God who has made His name dwell in this house will perform miracles for us at this time, even as God performed miracles for our ancestors in every generation. At that, a voice was heard out of the Holy of Holies, saying "The worship of idols in the Temple is nullified. Caligula has been slain, and his decrees nullified." The exact hour that these words were spoken was set down in writing.

When it became evident that Caligula's soldiers were coming closer to Jerusalem, one of the Jewish leaders said, "Go and meet them." As soon as the leader's word became known, all the Jewish notables gathered, went out to Caligula's legate and said, "All of us are prepared to die rather than have this decree imposed on us." As they kept crying aloud he responded, "Instead of crying aloud and beseeching a mere emissary, why don't you plead and cry aloud to your God in heaven to assist you?"

As the legate approached one city after another, he saw people coming toward him from each city. At the sight of them he was overwhelmed, saying, "How numerous they are." The informers told him, "These are Jews going out from each of the cities to confront you." However, when the legate came into each city, he saw men lying in sackcloth and ashes in its marketplaces.

No sooner did he reach Antipatris than a letter came informing him that Caligula had been assassinated and his decrees canceled. At that, the Jews seized the idols and dragged them through the streets. The day was declared a day of festivity (Talmud *Taanit* 11).

The Miraculous Space in the Temple

Though the people stood in close rows, they found ample space to prostrate themselves. Rabbi Aha said: "Each person had four cubits, a cubit on each side, so that no one should hear his neighbor's prayer" (Midrash Genesis Rabbah 5:7).

Miracle of the Fire of the Woodpile

It is taught: Five things were reported about the fire of the woodpile on the Temple altar: It lay like a lion, it was clear as the sun, its flame was a solid substance, it consumed freshly cut wood as though it were dry wood, and it caused no smoke to rise from it (Talmud *Yoma* 21b).

The Miracle of the Well in the Wilderness

The well that was with the Israelites in the wilderness had amazing properties. It resembled a rock the size of a beehive, from which, as out of a narrow jug, water coming out in a trickle shot high up into the air like a geyser. The well rolled up mountains with Israel and went down into valleys with them. . . . It branched out into streams so large that the Israelites would seat themselves in small boats and go visiting one another (Tosefta Sukkot 3:11–13; Numbers Rabbah 1:2).

The Miraculous Cloud of Glory

"And God went before them by day in a pillar of cloud to guide them" (Exodus 13:21). How many clouds of glory encompassed Israel in the desert? Seven clouds: one at each side of the four sides; one above them; one beneath them; and the one that advanced before them, raised every lowland, lowered each highland, and thus turned them all into level ground. As that cloud advanced, it also killed snakes and scorpions and swept and sprinkled the road before them (Mechilta, Beshallach, Vayechi, 1).

The Miracles of the Extended Day

Rabbi Nehemiah said in the name of Rabbi Mana: "Miracles occurred on that day. It was the eve of the Sabbath, and the inhabitants of all the cities assembled for the mourning over Rabbi. They set his body down in eighteen synagogues and then conveyed him to Bet Shearim. The day was extended for them so that each Israelite had time to arrive home, kindle the Sabbath light, roast the fish, and fill the cask with water before the Sabbath. When the last of them had done this, the sun set and the rooster crowed. The people began to cry out: 'Woe, we have desecrated the Sabbath.' A Heavenly Voice issued forth saying: 'Whoever did not stint himself in mourning for Rabbi is destined for the life of the World to Come, with the exception of Kazra who was there but did not accompany the funeral procession.' On hearing this, the man went up and threw himself from the roof and killed himself by the fall. A Heavenly Voice went forth and said: 'Also Kazra, for what he did on the roof, is destined for the life of the World to Come'" (Midrash Ecclesiastes Rabbah 9:3).

The Miraculous Water Stories

Rabbi Pinchas ben Jair went out into a place, and they said, "Our fountain no longer yields us water." He said, "Perhaps you are not particular about your tithes." They said, "Pledge yourself to us" [that if we do so, all will be well]. He pledged himself to them, and the fountain yielded its water.

Once Rabbi Pinchas was going to the House of Study and the Sinai river which he had to pass was so wide that he could not cross over it. He said: "O river, why do you prevent me from getting to the House of Study?" Then it divided its water, and he passed over. And his students said, "Can we also cross over it?" He said: "The person who knows that he has never insulted an Israelite can pass over it unharmed."

Rabbi Hegai in the name of Rabbi Nachman told this story. There was a righteous man who wanted to dig wells and cisterns for passers-by and travelers. One day his daughter, who was about to be betrothed, was drowned in a river. Everyone went to comfort him, but he would not receive their consolation.

Then Rabbi Pinchas went to console him, and he too was

not received. He said: "Is that your man of piety?" They said, "These are his deeds, and that is what befell him."

Then Rabbi Pinchas said: "Is it possible that he who has honored his maker through water would be overwhelmed in affliction through water?" Then the rumor ran through the city that the daughter had returned. Some said, "She was saved by a projecting peg." Others said that an angel came down in the likeness of Rabbi Pinchas and delivered her (Jerusalem Talmud Demai 1, 3).

Two Miracle Stories about the Heavenly Food Called Manna

a. Manna is described in the Bible as "bread," as "honey," and as "oil." How are the different descriptions to be reconciled? Young men tasted in it the taste of bread, old people the taste of honey, and infants the taste of oil (Midrash, Exodus Rabbah 25:3).

b. It is written: "When the dew fell in the camp at night, the manna fell upon it" (Numbers 11:9). It is also written, "The people shall go out and gather" (Exodus 16:4). And it is also written: "The people went about to and fro to gather it" (Numbers 11:8). How are the three statements to be reconciled? For the righteous, it came right down to the doors of the tents; ordinary people had to go out and gather it. But the wicked had to go about to and fro to gather it (Talmud *Yoma* 75a).

RABBINIC MIRACLE TALES OF ELIJAH

Elijah the Prophet is undoubtedly one of the most beloved characters in Jewish folklore and legend. Living in the 9th century B.C.E., he was a fiery preacher who often fought against cults and alien religious influences. Elijah was supposed to have his own court and legal problems which defied solution were to be referred to him (Talmud *Shekalim* 2:5 and *Bava Metziah* 3:4–5). Rabbis and men of great piety were said to have been guided by him in their studies. Nine legendary *beraitot* in the Talmud are introduced by the words, "It was taught at Elijah's school." In the late talmudic age Elijah becomes not only a precursor but an active partner of the Messiah. In the Midrash Leviticus Rabbah 34:8, both Elijah and the Messiah are busy recording the good deeds of the righteous. In the Talmud *Sotah* 9:15, Elijah is accorded the exclusive privilege of bringing about the resurrection of the dead. Because the Bible describes him as ascending to heaven in a fiery chariot rather than dying a death of a normal person, many miracle stories in rabbinic literature have been passed down through the generations. Recurrent themes in these stories include Elijah's ability to ward off the Angel of Death, blessing barren women and making them fertile, and acting as a provider, especially in his ability to make rain in time of drought. Since he did not die, many legends have him wandering the earth, often disguised as a poor person, a beggar, or a peasant. Here are nine miraculous Elijah tales in rabbinic writings.

The Fragrant Garment

Rabbah bar Abbuha met Elijah the Prophet and complained that his poverty was a bar to complete concentration of study. Elijah took him to the Garden of Eden and filled his pocket with leaves. As he was leaving, the Rabbi heard a voice say: "Rabbi bar Abbaha has already enjoyed his share in Paradise."

At once Rabbah emptied his pocket. When he was on earth again his garments bore a fragrance of the Garden of Eden, and he sold it for many thousands of dinars. He then distributed the money to his sons-in-law (Talmud *Bava Metziah*, 112).

Elijah Explains the Mysteries

Rabbi Joshua ben Levi fasted a long time and prayed that Elijah be revealed to him. Elijah appeared and in asking the Rabbi his wish, the latter replied: "To accompany you on your journeys throughout the world."

"On one condition," replied Elijah. "You must ask no questions. If you do, I shall leave at once."

They departed and went on their way until they arrived at a poor person's hovel. The owner welcomed them and offered them hospitality to the best of his ability. Before taking leave, Elijah placed his hand on the only cow that his host possessed, and it died immediately.

They went further and arrived at the home of a wealthy man. At first he refused to admit them, but after persuasion he allowed them to enter into the kitchen without offering them either food or drink. They noticed that one of the walls of his house was being repaired. Before they left, Elijah placed his hand on the wall, and it was completely restored.

Elijah and Rabbi Joshua went further and arrived at a house of study, where some rich people were listening to the discourse. After the discourse, they beheld the wanderers but paid little attention. They merely ordered the beadle to give them bread, salt, and water. After a moment, Elijah approached them and said: "May you all become chiefs."

The next morning Elijah and the Rabbi, continuing their travels, arrived at a town where they were given a warm welcome. Elijah blessed the people and said: "May only one of you become a chief."

Rabbi Joshua finally agreed to forgo Elijah's company and

asked him to explain everything. Elijah responded: "As for the poor man, the death of the cow was in place of his wife's predestined death. As for the rich man, I repaired the wall so that he might not find a treasure hidden there. As for the wealthy students of the Law, many chiefs will bring them to ruin. As for the good men of the city, one chief will bring them prosperity. This is the way that God works" (*Maassiot le-Rabbenu Nissim*).

Elijah Rescues Nachum ish Gam Zu

Nachum was a very pious man who would always say, no matter what happened to him, "This also is for the best" (in Hebrew, "Gam Zu letovah"). In this way he received his nickname.

It became necessary for the leaders of Palestine to send a gift to the Roman Emperor. Nachum was chosen as messenger in the expectation that God would grant success to a person that was so very righteous. For the gift he was given a jeweled box with gems. At a tavern while sleeping, the innkeeper emptied his guest's box and filled it with sand. When the Emperor's treasurer opened the casket, it was found to contain only sand. Nachum was then accused of disrespect for the Emperor and was sentenced to be executed. Even so, Nachum said: "This also is for the best."

God then sent Elijah in the guise of a Roman patrician who declared: "I have heard that there is a tradition among the Jews. When Abraham in his battle against the four kings was short of ammunition and his sword became dull, he threw sand at the enemy and it smote them like a sword. Let us try this sand. Perhaps it has the same property."

The execution was delayed and the sand was tested. The results were admirable. A town which had resisted the

Romans was now compelled to surrender under the impact of the sand. Nachum was released and his pockets filled with gold. He stopped at the same tavern and told the innkeeper of the gift he had received in exchange for what he had brought. The innkeeper carried a wagonload of sand to the palace but, when it was tested, it proved to be no different from any other sand. The innkeeper was executed for attempting to deceive the Emperor (Talmud *Taanit* 21a).

Elijah Saves Rabbi Shila

Rabbi Shila administered lashes to a man who had sexual intimacy with an Egyptian woman. The man informed against him to the government saying: "There is a man among the Jews who passes judgment without the permission of the government." An official was sent to summon him. When he came he was asked: "Why did you flog that man?" He answered: "Because he had intercourse with a female donkey." They said to him: "Do you have witnesses?" He replied: "I have." Thereupon Elijah came in the form of a man and gave evidence. They said to him: "If that is the case, he ought to be put to death." He replied: "Since we have been exiled from our land, we have no authority to put to death; do with him what you please."

While they were considering his case, Rabbi Shila exclaimed: "You, O God, are the greatness and the power" (I Chronicles 29:11). "What are you saying?" they asked him. He replied: "What I am saying is this: Blessed is the all-Merciful who has made the earthly royalty on the model of the heavenly, and has invested you with dominion, and made you lovers of justice." They then said to him, "Are you so solicitous for the honor of the government?" They gave him a staff and said to him: "You may act as judge" (Talmud *Berachot* 58a).

Elijah's Miraculous Rescue of Rabbi Kahana

Rabbi Kahana was selling baskets, when a certain matron made immoral demands upon him. He said to her: "I will first adorn myself." Thereupon he ascended and hurled himself from the roof towards the earth, but Elijah came and caught him. "You have troubled me to come four hundred parasangs," he reproved him. "What caused me to do it?" he retorted. "Is it not poverty?" So he gave him a shifra filled with denarii (Talmud *Kiddushin* 40a).

Elijah Cures a Toothache

Our teacher suffered a toothache for thirteen years, during which time no woman died in childbirth in Israel and no woman miscarried in Israel. At the end of the thirteen years, our Teacher once became angry with Rabbi Chiyya the Elder. Elijah of blessed memory visited our teacher in the guise of Rabbi Chiyya and laid his hand on his tooth, whereupon it was instantly cured! The next day Rabbi Chiyya visited him and asked him how his tooth was. "As soon as you put your hand on it yesterday it was cured," he answered him. At that Rabbi Chiyya exclaimed, "Woe to you, you women in childbirth and you pregnant women in Israel. Nevertheless, it was not I who laid my hand on your tooth." Our teacher then understood that it had been Elijah of blessed memory, and from that moment he began to show him honor (Midrash Genesis Rabbah 96:5).

The Wondrous Story of Beruria, Wife of Rabbi Meir

Beruria, the wife of Rabbi Meir, was a daughter of Rabbi Chanina ben Teradion. She said to her husband, "I am ashamed to have my sister placed in a brothel." So he took a tarkab-full of denarii and set out to release her. If, he thought, she has not been subjected to anything wrong, a miracle will occur for her, but if she has committed anything wrong, no miracle will occur.

Disguised as a knight, he came to her and said, "Prepare yourself for me." She replied, "The manner of women is upon me." "I am prepared to wait," he said. "But," she said, "there are many here that are prettier than I am."

He said to himself, this proves that she has not committed any wrong; she no doubt says thus to every comer.

He then went to her warder and said, "Hand her over to me." He replied, "I am afraid of the government."

He said, "Take the tarkab of dinars—one half distribute as a bribe, the other half shall be for yourself."

"What shall I do when these are exhausted?" he asked.

"Then," he replied, "say 'O God of Meir, answer me' and you will be saved."

"But," he said, "who can assure me that that will be the case?"

He replied: "You will see now." There were at that place some dogs who bit anyone who got them angry. He took a stone and hurled it at them, and when they were about to bite him he exclaimed, "O God of Meir, answer me," and they let him alone. The warder then handed her over to him. At the end the matter became known to the government, and the warder was taken up to the gallows, when he exclaimed, "O God of Meir answer me." They took him down and asked him what that meant, and he told them the incident that had happened. They then engraved Rabbi Meir's likeness on the gates of Rome and proclaimed that anyone seeing a person resembling the image should bring him there. One day some Romans saw Rabbi Meir and ran after him, so he ran away

from them and entered a harlot's house. Others say he
happened just then to see food cooked by heathens and he
dipped in one finger and then sucked the other. Others say
that Elijah the Prophet appeared to them as a harlot who
embraced them (Talmud *Avodah Zarah* 18b).

The Miraculous Spittle that Provides a Remedy from Sickness

Once Rabbi Meir was sitting and expounding, that a woman
went home, it being the Sabbath evening, and found that her
Sabbath light had been extinguished. Her husband asked her:
"Where have you been so late?" She replied: "I have been
listening to Rabbi Meir's discourse." Now that man, being a
scoffer, said to her: "You will not enter my house, whatever
happens, until you have gone and spat in the face of Rabbi
Meir."

   She left the house. Then Elijah, of blessed memory, appeared
to Rabbi Meir and said to him: "It is because of you that the
woman has left her house." Elijah, of blessed memory, then
acquainted Rabbi Meir with the episode. What did Rabbi
Meir do? He went and sat down in the great Bet HaMidrash.
That woman came in to pray, and on seeing her, Rabbi Meir
pretended to be blinking. He asked: "Who knows how to cure
a sore eye by a charm?" Whereupon the woman replied: "I
have come to cure it by charm." She spat in his face. Then he
said to her: "Tell your husband: 'I have spat in the face of
Rabbi Meir.'" He further said to her: "Go and become
reconciled with your husband. See how great is the power of
peace" (Midrash, Deuteronomy Rabbah 5:15).

Miracle of the Straw

Rabbi Akiva lived in great poverty before he became the
famous teacher. His rich father-in-law would have nothing to

do with him or his wife, because the daughter had married Akiva against her father's will. On a bitter cold winter night, Akiba could offer his wife, who had been accustomed to the luxuries that wealth can buy, nothing but straw as a bed upon which to sleep. He tried to comfort her with assurances of his love for the privations that she was suffering. At that moment Elijah appeared before the hut and cried out: "O good people, give me, I pray you, a little bundle of straw. My wife has been delivered of a child, and I am so poor that I do not even have enough straw to make a bed for her." Now Akiba could console his wife with the fact that their own misery was not so great as it might have been, and thus Elijah had attained his end, to sustain the courage of the pious (paraphrase, Talmud *Nedarim* 50a).

MIRACLES
IN JEWISH PHILOSOPHY

MEDIEVAL PERIOD

Saadia Gaon

The subject of miracles was an important one in the writings of medieval philosophers. Many of them found it difficult to accept the biblical notion of miracles. It was difficult to explain particular biblical miracles in terms of contemporary science but also because the acceptance of miracles entailed the belief in creation and divine providence—notions that were rejected by Greek philosophy.

Saadia ben Joseph, also known as Saadia Gaon because he was appointed head (Gaon) of the Sura Academy in Babylonia, may be considered the father of medieval philosophy. His philosophic system is fully expounded in his book *The Book of Beliefs and Opinions*. In it he does not question the possibility of miracles. Accepting the concepts of creation and divine providence, he is able to maintain that God may see fit to alter His creation in order to confirm His revelations to the prophets. In his *The Book of Beliefs and Opinions* (3:4,5), Saadia maintains that the purpose of miracles is to confirm the prophet as God's messenger whose word is truth. He also believes that a total correlation exists between the contents of revelation and the conclusions of rational investigation—God's existence, God's unity, and the creation of the world. However, the intellectual verification of revealed doctrines is accessible to few people, and therefore Saadia is of the opinion that revelation and miracles were required for the masses.

Allegorical interpretation of biblical miracles is perfected by Saadia, although the Midrash itself had already recorded many allegorical interpretations. While accepting the fact that every word of the Torah was divine, he insists that the truth of the Bible rests upon reason, and wherever the Bible seems to be in conflict with reason, the words must be taken in a metaphorical and allegorical sense. He therefore substitutes the speech of the angel for that of the serpent (Genesis 3:1) and of Bilaam's talking donkey (Numbers 22:28).

Regarding the understanding of the Torah text in general, Saadia argues that the text may be interpreted against its literal sense when it contradicts reason. All this is supported by proof or a validation by miracles. Prophets, for example, are required to validate their mission through the public display of miracles. This theory gave rise to Saadia's doctrine of tradition which states that there are three sources of knowledge: sense perception, rational self-evidence, and rational conclusions from data received by sense and reason. To this must be added the criterion of "reliable tradition." This belief in a reliable tradition provides the foundation for Saadia's notion of religious faith.

Judah HaLevi

HaLevi's teachings are based on the concept of immediate religious experience as being superior to deductive reasoning. Thus HaLevi defines the prophet as one who has attained the highest degree of perfection in conjunction with the perfection of the imaginative faculty. Although the intellectual might easily deny the possibility of the occurrence of miracles, the fact of miracles is upheld by the authenticity of the tradition which recorded it. Judah HaLevi does not, as did Saadia Gaon, regard the miracles as an affirmation of the content of revelation. Rather, he views the miracle as itself a direct revelation of God. God's direct communication with a person or a nation is a miracle. The deviation from the natural order for purposes of guiding humans to their religious destiny is a miracle. The authenticity of God's revelation at Mount Sinai was established by the fact that all of the Israelites— both children and adults—were granted prophecy along with Moses and could bear witness to that revelation out of their own personal experience.

In summation, for HaLevi biblical revelation is the source of religious truth, and since the Sinai revelation was a public act, it is beyond the possibility of error. Only the precise determination of the relationship between God and the individual is beyond what can be known by philosophy.

Maimonides

The greatest philosophic work written by Moses ben Maimon, also known as Maimonides, is *The Guide to the Perplexed*. This work was prepared to reconcile some of the differences between revelation and philosophy. As the title suggests, it is meant as a guide for those who have come to doubt either philosophy or religion as a result of this apparent contradiction. Maimonides considers neither to be alien to the other. Philosophy is the means through which the individual appropriates the content of revelation. And religious faith is a form of knowledge. Philosophy not only has religion as its object, but it is a central element in religion itself. Thus, the learning of philosophy is a religious task and philosophy paves the road to God.

According to Maimonides, miracles were predetermined at the time of creation and thus do not constitute a change in God's will or wisdom. They are necessary, in his opinion, to sustain the authority of revelation for the masses. Maimonides is very careful not to define the miracle as an abrogation of God's own laws of nature. Whenever a natural interpretation of a religious event seems sufficient and does not detract from the religious significance, Maimonides usually adopts it. He is also careful to prevent the affirmation of God's supernatural activity from becoming a means for the interruption of the natural order of creation. In his attempt to provide a rationalistic reason for the parting of the Red Sea, he explains that the nature of the water was not changed but rather affected by the forces of a strong wind. In other instances, he casts doubts on the Bible's account of miracles, often suggesting that what seems like a miracle was really a dream or a vision.

In his *Commentary on the Mishneh*, Maimonides teaches that the disposition for miracles was immersed in nature at the time of God's creation of the world. Both the regular processes of nature and the wondrous extraordinary ones were a part of God's plan for the beginning of creation.

In his *Guide to the Perplexed*, Maimonides no longer seems to hold to his extreme position, which would exclude any interference by God with the course of nature. He admits to the possible temporary suspension of the natural order of things as part of the Divinely conceived plan. Many miraculous biblical narratives, especially those that are most extraordinary such as Bilaam's talking donkey or the serpent's speech in the Garden of Eden, are explained by Maimonides allegorically or by interpreting the stories as part of the wild fantasy of prophetic imagination. When a prophet describes the ruin of a kingdom or the destruction of a great nation in expressions such as "the stars are fallen" or "the earth is waste and trembles," he speaks in metaphors alluding to the defeated. For them the light of the sun and the moon is darkened in the same sense that the victorious are said to enjoy light and gladness, while the defeated are in a state of darkness.

Speaking on the figurative language of the Bible, Maimonides in his *Guide to the Perplexed* cites Psalms 77:17–19, referring to the death of the Egyptians in the Red Sea: "The waters saw you and were afraid, the depths trembled . . . the earth shook and was confounded." Maimonides asserts that a miracle cannot prove what is impossible. It is useful only to confirm that which is possible (*Guide to the Perplexed* 3:24).

In summation, Maimonides posits that reality derives from divine reason and thus not everything imaginable is necessarily possible. He elevates the miracles of Moses above all of the others, while interpreting many biblical episodes allegorically which when taken literally become miraculous. Metaphysical truth comes through momentary flashes of illumination, something that is common to both philosophy and prophecy. Prophets often spoke in parable and metaphor because the typical individual could not comprehend truth in its purest form. Only the philosopher is capable of doing so, since metaphysical knowledge requires the perfection of the intellect and the purification of the human personality.

Gershon ben Levi

To explain the nature of miracles, Gershon ben Levi (known as Gershonides) examines the biblical miracles and found that they may be classified into those which involve a change of substance and those in which the substance remains the same. Examples of the former is the change of Moses' rod into a serpent and the Nile River turning into blood. An example of the latter was the hand of Moses becoming leprous. He further divides miracles into those where the prophet was told in advance (e.g., the ten plagues) and those where he was not (e.g., the reviving of the dead by Elijah). His examination of miracles shows that all were performed by prophets or in relation to them and that they were all done with some good purpose in mind. Since miracles did not appear accidental, they must, posits Gershon ben Levi, have as their author one who has knowledge—either God, the so-called Active Intellect (i.e., divine intelligence) or man (i.e., the prophet himself). He concludes that the author of miracles is the same as the inspirer of the prophets, whose intellect has as its content the unified system of sublunar creation as an immaterial idea (i.e., the Active Intellect). Thus for Gershon ben Levi, the prophet knows of the miracles because the Active Intellect, the author of them, is also the cause of the prophetic inspiration. This also accounts for the fact that all miracles have to do with events in the sublunar world and are not found in relation to heavenly bodies. Even the case of Joshua causing the sun and moon to stand still was no exception. There was really no standing still in this story. According to Gershon ben Levi, the expression in Joshua 10 that the sun and moon stood still means that the Israelites conquered the enemy in the short time that the sun occupied the zenith, while the motion was not noticeable for about an hour.

In all of his discussion of miracles, Gershon ben Levi shows a real attempt to minimize their extent and influence.

Nachmanides

During the life of Nachmanides there were philosophers who continued to repudiate the belief in miracles, explaining them as allegories, while others attempted to prove that they indeed did take place. Nachmanides, unlike Maimonides, suggests the miracle as preceding nature. Thus for Nachmanides the miracle is not a single occurrence but rather an unchangeable supranatural reality. According to Nachmanides, nature and worldly order do not affect the ends of the Torah, and therefore Israel's destiny is nothing short of miraculous. However, miracles do not necessarily conflict with the natural order. Nachmanides postulates a distinction between self-evident miracles (i.e., those which deviate from the natural order, serving to impart faith to unbelievers), and hidden miracles, which consist in the unusual coincidence of a number of natural events. The hidden miracles and their miraculous nature will be evident only to the believer.

Hasdai Crescas

Hasdai Crescas develops the most complete critique of Maimonides's position on miracles. Proposing that the world was created out of nothing but had no temporal beginning, the world is continually renewed by God's infinite grace. Since God is all-powerful and all-good, miracles (instruments of good) are not merely within God's power but a necessary effect of His very being and existence. For Crescas, miracles are neither a deviation of nature nor in conflict with it, but an expression of a supranatural order. Whereas natural occurrences are brought about by God indirectly, expressing a limited force, the miracle is brought about directly by God, expressing unlimited power and having an absolute existence. For Crescas, the world itself is actually a perpetual miracle which encompasses the natural order. The miracle precedes nature and its ultimate purpose is to impart faith to nonbelievers and to strengthen the faith of those who already believe.

For Crescas, in every event which the omnipotence of God is revealed, God becomes present to humans. Since God's grace is infinite, it must perforce reveal itself to all of humanity.

S. D. Luzzatto

Luzzatto is against the rational approach to religion and affirms the historicity of biblical miracles, including the miracle of prophecy itself. He proposes that miracles were the proof of divine providence.

Samuel Hirsch

This early nineteenth century philosopher also upheld the historicity of the miracles in the Bible. What was important for him and thus emphasized in his writings was not the miraculous event itself, but the educational value of the event. For example, in the biblical period, it was Hirsch's opinion that God revealed Himself to the people of Israel through miracles to demonstrate His supreme power over nature. Once the idea of the omnipotence of nature had been uprooted, miracles were no longer necessary, and, in fact, ceased to take place. According to Hirsch, the one single miracle that continues to take place up to the present time is the existence of the people of Israel, providing additional proof of God's existence.

Moses Mendelssohn

Mendelssohn holds that the truth of any religion cannot be maintained by appealing to miracles, but rather through the rationality of its doctrine. Once one's religious faith is upheld by reason, is it possible to consider the miracles associated with that religion? Mendelssohn does not reject the possibility of miracles, but rather emphasizes that Judaism did not appeal for belief to the authority of miracles but to that of direct revelation witnessed by the entire Israelite people.

CONTEMPORARY JEWISH PHILOSOPHERS AND MIRACLES

Franz Rosenzweig

Like Maimonides, Rosenzweig ascribes to a biblical conception of miracles based upon the idea that the miracle is a "sign" of God's presence. Rosenzweig affirms that miracles were built into the scheme of things from creation, and are thus a part of the natural order of the world. Attempting to connect science and miracles, or what he calls objectivity (i.e., idealism) and subjectivity (i.e., personal meaning), revelation for Rosenzweig becomes the point where the two are joined. The person who receives and lives a revelation carries both in him.

Abraham Joshua Heschel

For Heschel, a properly attuned person could conceivably consider any event a miracle in terms of personal meaning for him or her. Using terms such as "the legacy of wonder" and "radical amazement," he refers to the awe and wonderment that stirred the souls of humans.

Mordecai Kaplan

Using a rationalistic approach, Kaplan conceives the accounts of miracles as reflecting the attempt to prove and illustrate God's incredible power and goodness. He rejects the literalness of the miracle but sees the idea of responsibility and loyalty to what is right in the concept that God performs miracles for the sake of the righteous.

NOTABLE
MIRACLE QUOTATIONS

The following is a cross section of quotations culled from the Bible, Talmud, and the Midrash related to miracles. Reading them will help you to gain additional insight into the role of miracles in Jewish tradition.

1. "Miracles do not happen every day." (Talmud *Pesachim* 50b)
2. "Miracles do occur, but rarely do they provide food." (Talmud *Shabbat* 53b)
3. "Miracles do not take place on the hour." (Talmud *Megillah* 7b)
4. "A miracle cannot prove that which is impossible. It is useful only as a confirmation of that which is possible." (Maimonides, *Guide to the Perplexed*, 3)
5. "Believe in God through faith, and not because of miracles." (Nachman of Bratslav)
6. "Blessed be the Lord, the God of Israel, who alone does wondrous things." (Psalm 72:18)
7. "Whoever sees a place where miracles happened to

Israel must recite: Blessed be He who worked wonders for our ancestors in this place." (Talmud *Berachot* 54a)

8. Rabbi Yannai said: "One should never stay in a place of danger and say, 'I shall be saved by a miracle,' for perhaps no miracle will be brought, and even if one does occur, it will be deducted from his merits. Rabbi Chanan as proof of this quoted Genesis 32:11, 'I am not worthy of all the mercies [i.e., miracles] which you have done for me.'" (Talmud *Taanit* 20b)

9. "The person to whom a miracle happens is not aware of it himself." (Talmud *Niddah* 31)

10. "One who depends upon a miracle will experience none." (Sefer HaHinnuch)

11. Rabbi Alexandri said in the name of Rabbi Chiyya, "The miracle that occurs for a sick person is greater than the one brought for Hananiah, Mishael, and Azariah. The miracle for Hananiah, Mishael, and Azariah involved an ordinary fire lit by a human being, but the feverish fire of a sick person is from Heaven—who can extinguish that?" (Talmud *Nedarim* 41a)

12. "Miracles are not to be cited as an argument." (Talmud *Berachot* 60a)

13. "Where injury is likely, a person should not rely on a miracle." (Talmud *Kiddushin* 39b)

14. Rabbi Huna had wine stored in a building in need of repair. When he wanted to remove the wine, he took Rabbi Adda bar Ahavah into the building and kept him occupied in a learned discussion until the wine had been removed. Then, the moment they left the building, it collapsed. When Rabbi Adda realized that he had been used for such a purpose, he was annoyed, for he agreed with the view of Rabbi Yannai that a person

ought not to stay in a place of danger in the hope that a miracle will occur. (Talmud *Taanit* 20b)

15. "Is a blessing to be said only for a miracle occurring for many people, but not for one occurring for only one person? The answer: For a miracle that is brought for many people, it is the duty for everyone to say a blessing. For a miracle brought for one person, that person alone is required to say a blessing. If one sees the place where Israel crossed the Red Sea, or the place where Israel crossed the Jordan, or the place where Israel crossed the valleys of Arnon, or if one sees hailstones at the descent from Beth Horon, or the stone that Og King of Bashan wanted to throw at Israel, or the stone on which Moses sat while Joshua fought with Amalek, or the pillar of salt into which Lot's wife turned, or the wall of Jericho that was swallowed up into the ground upon which it stood—in each of these instances, one should utter thanksgiving and praise to God who is everywhere." (Talmud *Berachot* 54a)

16. Rabbi Pappa asked Abbaye: "Why were miracles performed for former generations, and no miracles are performed for us? Is it on account of learning?" In the days of Rabbi Judah, the sum of their learning was Nezikin, whereas we range over the entire six orders of the Mishneh. And when Rabbi Judah happened to reach the tractate of Uktzin, he would say in despair, "I find myself helpless in confronting the intricate theses of Rav and Samuel." Whereas, in matters of Uktzin, we on our own are able to advance thirteen ways of interpreting it. Nevertheless, Rabbi Judah had only to draw off one of his shoes and rain came, while we fast and cry out, but no one on High seems to need us.

Abaye replied: "Former generations gave up their lives for the hallowing of the Name. But we do not give up our lives for the hallowing of the Name." (Talmud *Berachot* 20a)

17. "And when Joseph's brothers saw that their father was dead, they said, 'It may be that Joseph bears a grudge against us' (Genesis 50:15). What did they see that made them afraid? As they were returning from burying their father, they saw that Joseph turned off the road and went to look at the pit into which his brothers had thrown him. Upon seeing this, he said, 'He still bears a grudge in his heart. Now that our father is dead, he will make his hatred of us felt.' But in reality Joseph's motive was a righteous one—he wanted to say a blessing for the miracle that occurred for him in that place." (*Tanchuma Vayechi* 17)

18. "Every favor which God performs for a person is a miracle." (Zohar 4, 200b)

19. "The belief in the hidden miracles is the basis for the entire Torah. A man has no share in the Torah, unless he believes that all things and all events in the life of the individual as well as in the life of society are miracles. There are no such things as the natural course of events." (Nachmanides)

20. "The greatest of all miracles is to bring into the heart of a Jew the holy influence whereby he may be enabled to pray properly to his Creator." (Rabbi Solomon of Karlin)

21. "It were evil indeed were we in our time in such a position that we required miracles to be shown to us." (The Gerer Rebbe)

22. "We rejoice in the existence of Medinat Yisrael (the State of Israel) in Eretz Yisrael (the Land of Israel) with

its capital of Jerusalem, the Holy City, the City of Peace. We view this phenomenon not just in political or military terms; rather, we consider it to be a miracle, reflecting Divine Providence in human affairs. We glory in that miracle; we celebrate the rebirth of Zion." (*Emet Ve-Emunah: Statement of Principles of Conservative Judaism*)

23. "The created world admits of no alteration of the natural law. God's miracles must be seen as if the world at that moment was in a state of original creation, and no alteration was involved." (Kedushat Levi)

24. "Nothing in the miracle of revelation is novel, nothing is the intervention of sorcery in created creation, but rather it is wholly sign, wholly the process of making visible and audible the providence which had originally been concealed in the speechless night of creation, wholly—revelation." (Franz Rosenzweig)

25. "On the six weekdays, the soul of the enlightened mediates on mundane affairs. But on the Sabbath, it must meditate to understand the works of God and His miracles." (Abraham ibn Ezra)

MIRACLES IN SHORT STORY

OPENING YOUR EYES

hen the people of Israel crossed through the Red Sea, they witnessed a great miracle. Some say it was the greatest miracle that ever happened. On that day they saw a sight more awesome than all the visions of the prophets combined. The sea split and the waters stood like great walls, while Israel escaped to freedom on the distant short. Awesome. But not for everyone.

Two people, Reuven and Shimon, hurried along among the crowd crossing through the sea. They never once looked up. They noticed only that the ground under their feet was still a little muddy—like a beach at low tide.

"Yucch!" said Reuven, "there's mud all over this place!"

"Blecch!" said Shimon, "I have muck all over my feet!"

"This is terrible," answered Reuven. "When we were slaves in Egypt, we had to make our bricks out of mud, just like this!"

"Yeah," said Shimon. "There's no difference between being a slave in Egypt and being free here."

And so it went, Reuven and Shimon whining and complaining all the way to freedom. For them there was no
miracle. Only mud. Their eyes were closed. They might as
well have been asleep (*Exodus Rabbah* 24:1).

People see only what they understand, not necessarily what
lies in front of them. For example, if you saw a television set,
you would know what it was and how to operate it. But
imagine someone who had never seen a television. To such a
person it would be just a strange and useless box. Imagine
being in a video store, filled with movies and stories and
music, and not even knowing it. How sad when something is
right before your eyes, but you are asleep to it. It is like that
with our world too.

Something like this once happened to Jacob, our father. He
dreamed of a ladder joining heaven and earth. Upon it angels
were climbing up and down. Then God appeared and talked
to Jacob. When he awoke the next morning, Jacob said to
himself, "Wow! God was in this very place all along, and I
didn't even know it!" (*Genesis* 28:16).

Rabbi Shelomo Yitzchaki, who lived in France eight hundred
years ago and whom we call Rashi (after the initials of his
name), explained what Jacob meant: "If I had known that
God would be here, then I wouldn't have gone to sleep!"

To be a Jew means to wake up and to keep your eyes open
to the many beautiful, mysterious, and holy things that
happen all around us every day. Many of them are like little
miracles: when we wake up and see the morning light, when
we taste food and grow strong, when we learn from others and
grow wise, when we hug the people we love and feel warm,
when we help those around us and feel good. All these and

more are there for us every day, but we must open our eyes to see them; otherwise we will be like Reuven and Shimon, able to see only mud.

Suppose, right now, your eyes are closed. How do you wake up?

MIRACLES ALL AROUND

There once was a man named Nahum Gam zu Letova, which means, "This, too, is for the best." People called him that because, no matter what happened to him, whether it was for good or for evil, he would always say, "*Gam zu letova*. This is also for the best." When he said those words, they sounded like a little prayer, and they would keep Nahum from becoming overly joyful or envious, upset or angry. Soon everyone began calling him Nahum Gamzu.

During the reign of the Roman emperor Caesar, the Jews decided to send a gift to him. Perhaps, they thought, the emperor would remember this gift and act more kindly toward the Jews in times of trouble. But who should be the one to deliver this gift? The rabbis decided that none other than Nahum Gamzu should be the one to present the gift.

The Jews, poor though they were, gathered together precious jewels, wrapped them in fine handwoven cloths, and put them in a chest. Then Nahum started on his journey to the emperor's palace. In the evening, he stopped at an inn.

As he was sleeping, some of the townspeople stole the contents of the chest and filled it with earth so he would not notice the theft when he lifted it in the morning.

When morning came, Nahum opened the chest to make certain everything was in order. When he saw the earth in place of the precious stones, he said aloud to himself, "*Gam zu letova*. This, too, is for the best." And Nahum took the chest, undisturbed, and continued on his way to the palace.

When he reached the palace and came before the emperor, Nahum placed the chest before him and said, "This is a gift from the Jews. Let this also be for the best."

The emperor signaled to his servants to open the chest.

When the cover was lifted, the emperor saw nothing but the earth. His advisors sifted their hands through the earth, looking for the hidden treasure. After all, who brings only earth to an emperor? But when the advisors found nothing of value, they said, "Your Majesty, the Jews are making a mockery of your royal dignity. Put this man to death."

At that moment, the Prophet Elijah appeared in the guise of one of the emperor's advisors, and he spoke out. "O King, this earth *may* hold great value for you. Perhaps it is part of the earth used by Abraham, the beloved of God, earth that became *transformed* into swords and arrows when it was thrown before the enemy. Remember that the Hebrews captured cities with this earth. Why not try it and test its worth *before* you kill this innocent man?"

The emperor listened and, after a while, said, "Very well, I accept your counsel. There is a city I have been unable to capture for some time now. Let us use it to find out if this earth has the magical qualities of ancient times."

The soldiers took the earth and threw some of it in the air toward the city. The earth turned into swords and spears and arrows, and the emperor was able to capture the city.

Overjoyed by his victory, the emperor ordered that the chest be filled with precious jewels as his gift to the Jews, and he gave Nahum a magnificent robe as a reward.

Nahum left the palace and, on his way home, he stopped at the same inn.

The thieves were surprised to see Nahum and *especially* to see him return with so much honor and reward. Since they were curious as to what had happened at the palace, they asked Nahum to tell them about his journey.

Nahum told them, "I brought the emperor a chest filled with earth. And he was so pleased with my gift that he gave me these jewels and a special royal robe."

On hearing this, what did those thieves do? They took several chests, filled them with the same earth they had put into Nahum's chest, and brought those chests to the emperor. "O Emperor, we bring you the same earth that the Jews sent you."

The thieves were already picturing themselves in royal robes, carrying home chests full of gold and precious jewels.

The emperor commanded, "Test this earth." But when the soldiers threw the earth into the air, it remained earth and only fell back to the ground.

Then the emperor ordered that the thieves be put to death and buried in that same earth.

As for our friend, Nahum, well, he continued to say "*Gam zu letova*" for the rest of his days.

Gam zu letova!

ELIJAH AND THE THREE WISHES

When Elijah the Prophet wanted to see how the people were behaving in a certain town, he would disguise himself as a beggar and walk around its streets. He would observe how the people were acting toward each other in the shops, in the parks, in the marketplace, in the synagogue. As he walked, he would blink his eyes, nod his head, shrug his shoulders, stroke his long white beard, or tap his walking stick as though he were recording what he saw, adding that message to the already bulging sack he carried over his shoulder. He often smiled to himself, too, while humming a melody as he walked from place to place.

One day, he noticed a small cottage. "This place needs a great many repairs," he observed. "A new roof, better window shutters, a gate. Yet here are some beautiful flowers growing in the tiny front yard. Hollyhocks, poppies, a mandrake plant. I like that!" Weary from traveling, and hungry too, Elijah decided to stop at this house to rest a while. He knocked on the door.

In this cottage, there lived a poor man and his wife. The man came to the door. When Elijah asked him for some water to drink, the man invited him in. Seeing how hungry and tired this traveler was, the couple asked him to say and share their meal.

"Come and eat with us," said the good wife. "Eating with a guest makes the meal feel like a banquet, even though we cannot offer you more than the little we have."

"Come," said her husband. "We will gladly share whatever we have." The couple offered him what they had prepared for their dinner. There was a small piece of herring and a thick slice of black bread, and some water to drink. The meal was hardly enough even for the two of them.

When the stranger had eaten and was refreshed, he turned to the couple and said, "Because of your kindness to me, I will grant you any three wishes."

At first not believing what he had heard, the poor man just stood there quietly. Then he began to think to himself, "Let me test him to see if what this bedraggled traveler says is true. There is some mystery about him. Maybe God has answered our prayers to help us out of our hard times."

After a few minutes, the poor man replied, "This house needs so much repair and it is so tiny that I don't have room enough for my books. I would like to have a large house, like a palace."

Elijah whistled, and instantly a mansion appeared where the cottage had stood.

At that moment, the woman, looking down at her clothes and quickly taking off her old apron, exclaimed, "Oh, we should have beautiful clothes, with shining, glittering jewels," gesturing wildly as she pointed to her hair, ears, neck, and wrists. "We look so plain in this wonderful house," she explained.

Again Elijah whistled, and the couple was instantly dressed in clothes of velvet and satin, with magnificent diamond, pearl, and emerald jewelry covering the wife's head, ears, neck, and wrists.

"Gold!" they both shouted together with great excitement for their third wish.

Elijah whistled for the third time, and sacks of gold appeared. A moment later, Elijah disappeared.

Several years went by, and Elijah wanted to see how the good couple had fared. When Elijah appeared at the gate of their mansion, again disguised as a beggar, he looked around first. He saw heavy shutters on the windows and high fences around the house. While there was a great deal of land around the house, nowhere were there any flowers. As he stood looking through the gate, the servants, seeing this stranger through the watchman's door near the gate of the yard, would not let him stand there.

"I would like to see the master of the house," demanded Elijah. The servants laughed and brought the dogs closer to the gate, signaling the beggar to leave. The master of the house himself came to the door to see what the commotion was. Since he did not recognize the beggar, he shouted orders for the beggar to leave or be chased away.

Disappointed and saddened by what he had seen, Elijah whistled once and the gold disappeared.

He gave another whistle, and the beautiful clothes and jewels vanished.

The Elijah gave a third whistle, and the mansion instantly turned back into the small cottage that had once before stood in that place.

In the same moment, the couple realized how selfish they had become. They understood then how poor they had been, even when they had all the riches in the world.

ELIJAH THE BUILDER

There once was a good, pious couple who had five children. But rich as they were in faith and family, so poor were they in wealth. Now the husband had not been able to find work for many weeks.

One day, when they did not have enough bread to put on the table, and the children cried from hunger, the wife said, "Husband, go to the marketplace. Maybe today God on High will help you find some work so you an earn a few pennies. We must not give up hope. God will help you, but not if you just sit at home."

And her husband answered, "Where can I go that I haven't been? What new doors can I knock on that I haven't tried? I have no rich relatives, no rich friends—not that I would bring shame on us by borrowing from anyone."

However, each day the situation became worse, and finally

the wife cried, "How can you sit and watch your children die before your eyes? Go, husband, trust in God. May God bring you hope so you may prosper."

Reluctantly, the husband left the house, walked a little way in one direction, then in another, and finally he sank to the ground, looked up at the heavens and prayed: "Great God in the heavens, great and good God. Take pity on us; have mercy on us. Our hunger is terrible and we ask, we plead with you, O Merciful God, You who created us, hear my prayers and turn to us in Your mercy and send Your help—or else let me die now and quickly, so I should no longer see how my children and wife suffer."

And then he rose and walked on as in a daze, weeping and praying. Suddenly, a young man appeared on the road, walking toward the unfortunate husband. He stopped and asked the unhappy man what troubled him so. And the man wept again, as he told his story of misery.

Then the young man, who was Elijah the Prophet in disguise, said, "Take me to the marketplace and sell me to the person I will point out to you. When you receive the agreed-upon price, give me one dinar. That is all you have to do."

"Good sir," said the astonished husband, "you are kind in offering to help, but you look more like my master and I your slave. They will never believe me when I look like this." And the man pointed to his rags and bare feet.

But Elijah insisted. "Do as I tell you, and all will be well with you. Come, and we'll go to the auction."

As they walked through the marketplace, many did mistake the man for Elijah's slave, but Elijah told them, "No, he is my master."

It happened that one of the King's ministers had come riding through to buy slaves for the building of the King's new palace. Upon seeing the strong young man, the minister began to bid for him as soon as Elijah was called up for sale. When the King's minister offered the price of 80 dinars, Elijah said quickly to the man. "Sell me to the one who bid 80 dinars, and do not accept any more bids." The man took the 80 dinars, and gave one dinar to Elijah as he had promised.

Elijah held the dinar in his hand for a moment and then said, "Take this dinar now and return home. May it be for good. You will never suffer from poverty or want again." And he blessed the man.

When Elijah rode off with the King's minister, the man bought all kinds of good food and returned home.

After his family had eaten, the wife said, "My husband, you did what I advised, and it seems as if I gave you good counsel. But tell me how this came to pass. How did you earn this money?" And her husband told her how he had met the young man and who he really was.

When Elijah left with the King's minister, he was brought to the King. The King had been planning to build a great palace outside the city and had bought many slaves to haul stones, timber, and other building materials. As soon as the King saw Elijah he asked, "And do you have a particular skill or shall we put you to work with all the slaves to drag stones and cut trees?"

"I am a builder, your Majesty," said Elijah, "and I can work best by planning and directing the work."

"Well then, it is our good fortune that we have purchased you today," said the King, and he explained his plan for the great palace he desired to have built. "Build it for me in six months' time, and I will reward you greatly and also grant you your freedom."

"Your Majesty," replied Elijah, "I will do as you ask in even a shorter time. Have the slaves prepare all the building materials at once."

The King directed all the slaves to do as Elijah had asked.

That night, Elijah prayed that God Most High perform a miracle and build the palace according to the King's wishes.

And a miracle happened. All the angels came down from the heavens and worked together to build a magnificent palace. As soon as it was dawn, the palace was finished and Elijah knew the King would be pleased. And when Elijah saw that the angels had finished their work and returned to the heavens, he, too, disappeared.

In the morning, the slaves arose for the day's work but, to their astonishment, they saw the completed palace. They ran to the King, who then searched for his chief builder.

"He must have been one of the angels," the King said when he could not find Elijah anywhere. "But," he added with a grand gesture as though speaking to the air, "I release you and declare you a free man!"

One day, Elijah met the man who had sold him, and the man asked him. "Tell me, how did you fare when you were brought to the King?"

And Elijah answered, "I could have freed myself immediately; but a promise is a promise, and he had paid good money for me to work. So I built him a great palace as he asked. I did not want him to regret buying me and paying so much gold. I performed a task for him worth many times over what he had paid for me. After I fulfilled my promise, I left."

Then the man understood that this was Elijah and thanked him many times and said, "You have restored us to life."

As time passed, the couple acquired even greater good fortune; and they were blessed for the rest of their lives, grateful to God Most High for all that they now had in their lives.

MIRACLES
IN THE PRAYERBOOK

"We thank you and praise you morning, noon and night for Your Miracles." (Amidah)

The prayerbook has its roots in both the biblical and ancient rabbinic texts which constitute the core of every worship service. Passages from the Five Books of Moses, from the Book of Psalms and from the Prophets, among other biblical sources, were arranged for prayer by the ancient rabbis of the first through the sixth centuries.

The Hebrew word for miracle, *nes*, does make several appearances in the prayerbook, both in the sense of a supernatural event that God has performed for humanity as well as in the sense of the daily wonder of life. This chapter will summarize those prayers which reflect both nuances of the miracle and the ways in which the liturgy expresses them.

MODEH ANI: THE MIRACLE OF AWAKENING EACH DAY

In the opening section of the daily morning services there are several prayers that celebrate the renewal of life in a new day, considered to be one of the so-called hidden miracles.

Worshippers need to be constantly reminded of them in order to better appreciate them. The very opening prayer of the prayerbook, *Modeh Ani* ("we give thanks"), says the following: "I am grateful to you, living and enduring Sovereign One, for restoring my soul to me in compassion. You are faithful to me beyond measure."

This prayer thanks God each day for renewing one's physical and mental abilities, praising God for the wonder of being able to lie dormant during sleep and awaken each morning to the renewal of a day. In addition it praises God for His extraordinary dependability in maintaining a regular and orderly cycle of nature. It seems quite obvious that it was the intention of this prayer to remind the worshipper daily that the routine act of awakening after hours of sleep is something that humans should not take for granted.

ASHER YATZAR: PRAYER OF APPRECIATION FOR ONE'S BODILY FUNCTIONS THAT WORK WONDROUSLY

This ancient prayer, appearing in the very early part of the prayerbook, is said privately by each worshipper before the start of the service. According to Jewish tradition, it is also customarily recited each time one finishes using the bathroom. The prayer praises God for creating the wondrous mechanism of the human body which allows for the elimination of wastes and the preservation of the body. It is again a reminder not to take for granted even the routine act of going to the bathroom and that the marvelous way in which one's body functions is due to the magnificent ability of God the creator. Here is the prayer:

Praised are You, Lord our God, Ruler of the Universe, who with wisdom fashioned the human body, creating openings, arteries, glands and organs, marvelous in design. Should but one of them by being blocked or opened not work properly, it would be impossible to exist. Praised are You, God, Healer of all flesh who sustains our bodies in wondrous ways.

BARUCH SHE'AMAR: BLESSED BE GOD WHO SPOKE AND THE WORLD CAME INTO BEING

This prayer, a litany of praises to God, begins by praising God for having created the world using only the spoken word: "Blessed be God who spoke, and the world came into being." Whereas in other Near Eastern creation stories the gods created the world using a variety of props, the One God of the Israelites is appreciated in this prayer for having created the world out of nothing by saying words that caused the world to come into being. The prayer is thus a constant reminder to the daily worshipper that God's world is wondrous and God's creative powers are marvelous, making possible all that humans see and experience each and every day.

ASHRAY: PSALM 145

The Talmud (*Berakhot* 4b) states that "whoever says this prayer three times each day will be assured of a place in the world-to-come." The explanation often given for this unusual statement is the fact that within the prayer is the following verse: "You open your hand O God and satisfy all living things with favor." Here, God is recognized for being the ultimate source in the maintenance of all of life. The worshipper is made to appreciate the "miracle" of God's sustaining powers. Within the prayer there is an allusion to the miracle in the following verse: "They tell of your wonders and of your glorious splendor." Although the "wonders" in this verse are not defined, they clearly seem to point to all the wondrous and extraordinary acts God has performed and will continue to perform in human history to sustain the world. These acts, as further defined in Psalms 146–150 which follow in the prayerbook, include the following: bringing justice to the oppressed, protecting the stranger (Psalm 146), healing the broken-hearted, providing rain for the earth and food for beasts (Psalm 147), and the ability for natural phenomena such as fire, snow, and storms to obey God's command (Psalm 148).

SONG OF THE SEA

The Song of the Sea is the victory song that Moses and the Israelites sang after crossing the Red Sea. After the destruction of the Jerusalem Temple this song, consisting of verses 1–18 of the fifteenth chapter of the Book of Exodus, was introduced into the daily morning liturgy. It praises God for perhaps the greatest miracle in recorded history—splitting the Red Sea, allowing the Israelites to safely cross while the Egyptians who followed drowned. Here are some verses from this prayer that describe the miracles:

> I will sing to God, mighty in majestic triumph,
> Horse and rider He has hurled into the sea.

> The Lord is my strength and my might; He is my
>   deliverance. . . .
> In the rush of the rage the waters were raised
> The sea stood motionless, the great deep congealed. . . .

It is clear that for the Israelites the splitting of the Red Sea demonstrated God's miraculous might and power, not to mention His caring relationship with Israel. The recitation of this prayer is meant to be a constant reminder of God's ability to cause wondrous acts on behalf of his beloved people. It should also be noted that the liberation from Egyptian slavery was considered such a wondrous act that there are over 40 references to it throughout the Jewish liturgy.

L'EL BARUCH

This prayer with its blessing of light that precedes the Shema proclaims that God is the Sovereign of wonders (i.e., miracles). It seems clear from this prayer that the wonders referred to here are the hidden miracles of everyday life, since the reference to God as Sovereign of wonders is immediately followed by the statement that God daily renews His creation. Here is a portion of the prayer:

> Awesome in praise, Sovereign of wonders, day after day in His goodness He renews creation. So sang the Psalmist: Praise the Creator of great lights, for His love endures forever. Cause a new light to illumine Zion and may we all soon share a portion of its radiance. Praised are You, God, Creator of lights.

MI KAMOCHA:
WHO IS LIKE UNTO YOU, O GOD

The words of this prayer (Exodus 15:11) are actually a part of the Song of the Sea. In a sense, it forms the climactic ending of the Song, asking the rhetorical question "Who is like You, O God, among all that is worshipped? Who is like you, majestic in holiness, awesome in splendor, working wonders [i.e., miracles]?" These words, recited in each of the three daily services, help to provide a constant reminder to the worshipper that God is holy, dependable, and truly worthy of praise because He is a God who can perform wonders.

AMIDAH: THE STANDING PRAYER

The Amidah is a prayer that is central to the Jewish liturgy and is included in varying forms in every prayer service. In the daily Amida there are 19 blessings, several of which relate God's miraculous power. For example, in the second blessing of the Amidah which appears in the "Gevurot" ("Power") section, God's power is described as follows: "You give life to the dead, great is your saving power. . . . What power can compare with yours? You are the master of life and death in deliverance."

Here in these verses God's amazing power extends to giving life to the dead!

In the eighteenth blessing of the Amidah, in the section called "Hoda'ah" ("Thanksgiving"), God is given thanks for the daily miracles of life. This is one of the few times in the prayerbook that the Hebrew word for miracle (*nes*) is actually used:

We proclaim that You are the Lord our God and God of our ancestors throughout all time. You are the Rock of our lives, the Shield of our deliverance in every generation. We thank You and praise You morning, noon and night for Your miracles which daily attend us and for Your wondrous kindnesses.

The Amidah also affords the worshipper an opportunity to add a special paragraph to be said on the holidays of Hanukkah and Purim. Both of these paragraphs include an opening line thanking God for His miraculous deliverance during a time of grave peril. In the case of Hanukkah, the Jews were persecuted by the Syrian-Greeks who were defeated by a small but persistent army of Maccabee soldiers. In the Purim story, the Jews were threatened with total annihilation by the malevolent Haman and miraculously saved by Queen Esther using her wit, charm, beauty, and God's assistance behind the scenes. Here is the opening verse of the paragraph known in Hebrew as "al ha-nissim" ("for the miracles"). Once again the word for miracle appears in this verse: "We thank You for the miraculous deliverance, for the heroism and for the triumphs in battle of our ancestors in other days, and in our time."

PRAYER ANNOUNCING
THE NEW MONTH

In the prayer that is said on the Sabbath preceding a new month in the Jewish calendar, God is petitioned to grant a long and peaceful life to all people. This is followed by a paragraph which petitions God for the ingathering of the exiled people of the world. In this paragraph there is a reference to the miracles that God brought for our ancestors. The actual Hebrew word for miracle—*nes*—again appears in the plural form *nissim*: "May God who brought miracles for our ancestors, redeeming them from slavery to freedom redeem us soon and gather our dispersed from the four corners of the earth."

PRAYERBOOK BLESSINGS

Blessings were said to have been created by the men of the Great Assembly who lived approximately 400–300 B.C.E. Many of the blessings created to be used in daily life were intended to express praise of God and appreciation for natural phenomena of everyday life that are amazing, awesome, and beautiful, but often go unnoticed because of the hurried pace of society. In philosophical times these miracles of life, which are to be responded to by offering God a blessing, are the so-called daily hidden miracles. Here is a sampling of them:

On Seeing a Rainbow: *Baruch atah Adonai elohaynu melech ha'olam zocher ha-berit ve'ne'eman bivrito vekayam be'ma'amaro.* Praised are You, God, who remembers the covenant and is faithful in keeping promises.

On Seeing Trees Blossoming for the First Time in the Year: *Baruch atah Adonai elohaynu melech ha'olam shelo chisar b'olamo davar uvara vo briyot tovot v'ilanot tovim l'hanot bahem b'nai adam.* Praised are You, God, who has withheld nothing from the world and has created lovely creatures and beautiful trees for people to enjoy.

On Seeing Trees or Creatures of Unusual Beauty: *Baruch atah Adonai elohaynu melech ha'olam shekacha bo b'olamo.* Praised are You, God, who has such beauty in the world.

On Seeing Lightning, Shooting Stars, Mountains, or Sunrises: *Baruch ata Adonai elohaynu melech ha'olam oseh ma'asey b'reshit.* Praised are You, God, Sovereign of the Universe, Source of Creation.

On Hearing Thunder: *Baruch ata Adonai elohaynu melech ha'olam she'kocho u'gevurato malay olam.* Praised are You, God, whose mighty power fills the entire world.

For Further Reading

Balter, Henry, trans. *The Treatise Ta'anit*. Philadelphia: Jewish Publication Society, 1967.

Buber, Martin. *I and Thou*. New York: Scribner, 1958.

Glatzer, Nahum. *Franz Rosenzweig: His Life and Thought*. New York: Schocken, 1973.

Guttmann, Julius. *The Philosophy of Judaism*. New Jersey: Jason Aronson, 1988.

Heschel, Abraham Joshua. *Between God and Man*. New York: The Free Press, 1959.

Husik, I. *A History of Medieval Jewish Philosophy*. New York: Harper and Row, 1966.

Kaplan, Mordecai. *The Greater Judaism in the Making: A Study of the Modern Evolution of Judaism*. New York: Jewish Reconstructionist Press, 1960.

———. *Judaism Without Supernaturalism*. New York: Jewish Reconstructionist Press, 1958.

Maimonides, Moses. *Guide for the Perplexed*. Translated by S. Pines. Chicago: University of Chicago Press, 1956.

Neusner, Jacob. ed. *Understanding Jewish Theology*. New York: Ktav Publishers, 1973.

Schram, Peninnah. *Jewish Stories One Generation Tells Another*. New Jersey: Jason Aronson, 1987.

INDEX

About the Author

Rabbi Ronald Isaacs is the rabbi of Temple Sholom in Bridgewater, New Jersey. He received his doctorate in instructional technology from Columbia University's Teacher's College. He is the author of numerous books, including *Loving Companions: Our Jewish Wedding Album*, coauthored with Leora Isaacs; *Words for the Soul: Jewish Wisdom for Life's Journey*, and *Mitzvot: A Sourcebook for the 613 Commandments*. Rabbi Isaacs is currently on the Publications Committee of both the Rabbinical Assembly and C.A.J.E. and also serves on the editorial board of *Shofar* Magazine. He resides in New Jersey with his wife, Leora, and their children Keren and Zachary.